Techniques for Reading Assessment and Instruction

Techniques for Reading Assessment and Instruction

Barbara J. Walker
Oklahoma State University

PEARSON

Merrill
Prentice Hall

Upper Saddle River, New Jersey
Columbus, Ohio

Library of Congress Cataloging-in-Publication Data

Walker, Barbara J.
    Techniques for reading assessment and instruction / Barbara J. Walker.
        p. cm.
    Includes bibliographical references and index.
    ISBN 0-13-191360-3
        1. Reading—Remedial teaching. 2. Reading—Ability testing. I. Title.

LB1050.5.W363 2005
372.43—dc22

2004044620

Vice President and Executive Publisher: Jeffery W. Johnston
Senior Editor: Linda Ashe Montgomery
Editorial Assistant: Laura J. Weaver
Production Coordination: Lea Baranowski, Carlisle Publishers Services
Production Editor: Linda Hillis Bayma
Design Coordinator: Diane C. Lorenzo
Cover Designer: Terry Rohrbach
Cover Image: Scott Cunningham/Merrill
Production Manager: Susan Hannahs
Director of Marketing: Ann Castel Davis
Marketing Manager: Darcy Betts Prybella
Marketing Coordinator: Tyra Poole

This book was set in Garamond by Carlisle Communications, Ltd. It was printed and bound by R.R. Donnelley & Sons Company. The cover was printed by Coral Graphic Services, Inc.

This book is derived from *Diagnostic Teaching of Reading: Techniques for Instruction and Assessment,* 5th edition, by Barbara J. Walker, © 2004. Used by permission of Pearson Education, Inc., Upper Saddle River, NJ.

Pearson Education Ltd.   Pearson Education Australia Pty. Limited
Pearson Education Singapore Pte. Ltd.   Pearson Education North Asia Ltd.
Pearson Education Canada, Ltd.   Pearson Educación de Mexico, S.A. de C.V.
Pearson Education—Japan   Pearson Education Malaysia Pte. Ltd.

10 9 8 7 6 5 4 3 2 1
ISBN: 0-13-191360-3

*To my Mom and Dad, Helen and Frank Shell,
for their support and encouragement
through the years*

About the Author

Barbara J. Walker is professor of reading at Oklahoma State University where she teaches courses in reading difficulties and coordinates the Reading and Math Center. Dr. Walker received her Ed.D. from Oklahoma State University in Curriculum and Instruction, specializing in reading difficulty. Prior to returning to Oklahoma, Dr. Walker was a professor in the Department of Special Education and Reading at Montana State University, Billings, where she coordinated the Reading Clinic. She was a reading specialist in the elementary schools of Stillwater, Oklahoma; organized and taught the college reading program at Vernon Regional Junior College in Vernon, Texas; and coordinated the educational program at the Hogar Paul Harris in Cochabamba, Bolivia.

Dr. Walker's research interests focus on teacher development, early literacy intervention, and reading difficulties. Her publications include *Diagnostic Teaching of Reading: Techniques for Instruction and Assessment* (4th ed.), *Supporting Struggling Readers* (2nd ed.), *Training the Reading Team* with Ronald Scherry and Lesley Morrow, *Tips for the Reading Team* and *The Reading Team: A Handbook for K–3 Volunteer Tutors* with Lesley Morrow, and *Interactive Handbook for Understanding Reading Diagnosis* with Kathy Roskos. She is currently coeditor of *Literacy Cases Online,* a publication of the College Reading Association. Dr. Walker received the College Reading Association's 1997 A. B. Herr Award for outstanding contributions to reading education and was a distinguished finalist for the International Reading Association's 1991 Albert J. Harris Award for research in reading disabilities.

Dr. Walker is a state, national, and international professional leader, having served on the board of directors of the International Reading Association, the College Reading Association, and the Montana State Reading Council. Most important to her, however, is preparing teachers to work with struggling readers. In this capacity, she has helped more than 2,500 struggling readers improve their literacy.

Preface

Teachers are perceptive educators and reflective thinkers who make sophisticated decisions about instructional interactions on a daily basis. They realize that no one approach is better than others in all literacy situations and with all learners. In fact, they understand that the students in their classrooms are unique and respond differently to instructional techniques. This book is grounded in the belief that, as a nation, our strengths lie in our individual differences. These differences need to be nurtured through instruction, and instruction should build on the unique strengths of each student.

This book was designed to be used by classroom teachers, reading tutors, and reading specialists in educational environments. It is hoped that teachers will use it when they are seeking ways to meet individual students' strengths and needs.

Organization of the Text

Part One of this text describes aspects of teaching and assessing reading as well as information about literacy learning and its influence on instruction. Chapter 1, "Teachers as Problem Solvers," looks at perspectives about reading and reading instruction. Chapter 2, "The Roles of Effective Teachers," discusses the responsibilities teachers assume as they coach student learning, while Chapter 3, "A Framework for Teaching Reading," provides a suggested outline for teaching reading. Chapter 4, "Gathering Assessment Data," provides information about evaluating the student while Chapter 5, "Selecting Instructional Techniques," provides charts that help teachers select techniques to promote learning growth.

Part Two presents simple descriptions and procedures for 55 instructional techniques. Following each description, the view of reading underlying each technique is described, and information is provided to indicate when to use the technique for optimum effectiveness in teaching reading.

Acknowledgments

This book represents a view of learning that was developed over years of experience. I am grateful to many individuals who have supported my learning. I particularly want to thank my mother and father, Helen and Frank Shell, for instinctively modeling how to be an innovative thinker and enduring learner. As I grew up, they encouraged me to express my individuality and follow my dreams. My own children, Chris and Sharon Walker, have been a constant reminder that learning occurs differently for each individual. I thank them for showing me how they learn in their unique ways. I am indebted to Darrell (Pete) Ray, my mentor, for initiating my quest to understand individual differences in learning to read. Special thanks are extended to Linda Montgomery for conceptualizing the format of this book. I also want to thank Linda Bayma and Lea Baranowski for their tireless efforts to create my image of how the information should be presented.

Adjusting instruction to meet the changing needs and strengths of students is a challenging yet rewarding task. This book is intended to facilitate instructional decision making in classrooms and tutoring programs.

Educator Learning Center:
An Invaluable Online Resource

Merrill Education and the Association for Supervision and Curriculum Development (ASCD) invite you to take advantage of a new online resource, one that provides access to the top research and proven strategies associated with ASCD and Merrill—the Educator Learning Center. At **www.EducatorLearningCenter.com** you will find resources that will enhance your students' understanding of course topics and of current educational issues, in addition to being invaluable for further research.

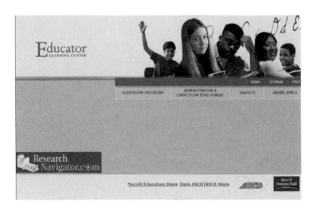

How the Educator Learning Center Will Help Your Students Become Better Teachers

With the combined resources of Merrill Education and ASCD, you and your students will find a wealth of tools and materials to better prepare them for the classroom.

Research

- More than 600 articles from the ASCD journal *Educational Leadership* discuss everyday issues faced by practicing teachers.
- A direct link on the site to Research Navigator™ gives students access to many of the leading education journals, as well as extensive content detailing the research process.
- Excerpts from Merrill Education texts give your students insights on important topics of instructional methods, diverse populations, assessment, classroom management, technology, and refining classroom practice.

Classroom Practice

- Hundreds of lesson plans and teaching strategies are categorized by content area and age range.
- Case studies and classroom video footage provide virtual field experience for student reflection.
- Computer simulations and other electronic tools keep your students abreast of today's classrooms and current technologies.

Look into the Value of Educator Learning Center Yourself

A four-month subscription to Educator Learning Center is $25 but is **FREE** when used in conjunction with this text. To obtain free passcodes for your students, simply contact your Merrill/Prentice Hall sales representative, and your representative will give you a special ISBN to give your bookstore when ordering your textbooks. To preview the value of this website to you and your students, please go to **www.EducatorLearningCenter.com** and click on "Demo."

Brief Contents

Contents

Part One

Teaching Reading to Learners Who Find Reading Challenging   1

Part Two

Instructional Techniques 95

Techniques

Teaching Reading to Learners Who Find Reading Challenging

Part One of this book outlines the teaching process (Chapter 1) and its use with children who find reading challenging. Teachers collect data about students as readers and writers (Chapter 3) and use this data to design instructional routines (Chapters 2 and 3). The students are viewed as active learners who build a model of meaning as they read and write. As children read and write, they are influenced by many factors, including the text, the task, the technique, their own strategies and approaches, and other social factors like group membership.

Teachers must continually evaluate the influence these multiple factors have on children's literacy behaviors and plan effective instruction accordingly (Chapter 2). Teachers orchestrate many facets that influence children as they interact during literacy events. Thus a teacher is purposeful in providing a supportive instructional context for children. By using the instructional framework provided in Chapter 3 and by gathering student data, teachers can feel confident in selecting instructional techniques that align with individual student needs.

The teacher's role is to encourage readers to use both what they know and the text to construct meaning within the social context (Chapter 1). In the first part of this book, reading theories are discussed. The point of view of this book is that readers are active and constructive as they approach learning tasks. Although a teacher may select instructional techniques and materials that are based in other theories, an informed teacher strives to balance his instruction within the active reading framework.

Ways to Use These Chapters

Chapters 1 and 2 can provide a conceptual and theoretical basis for the subsequent chapters in this section. The information in Chapter 2 can be used as a checklist for teaching behaviors. Often, teachers make a self-assessment measure using the guidelines in Chapter 2 in order to evaluate their own performance. Likewise, they make a mental checklist of aspects of lesson planning found in Chapter 3. Further, they use the information in Chapter 3 to design instruction with a struggling reader. Using this framework (familiar text time, guided contextual reading, strategy and skill instruction, and personalized reading and writing) provides a balanced approach to instruction.

Using the information in Chapter 4, the teacher designs assessments, including the following: the use of an informal reading inventory and other skill assessments like letter identification, phonemic segmentation, and fluency assessments. The teacher then carefully selects additional assessments that will augment instructional decision making. Finally, teachers can use Chapter 5 to select techniques to use during the lesson framework. By using the charts in Chapter 5, the teacher can readily select instructional techniques based on the analysis of assessment data and observations during teaching. If the teachers are searching for a technique for guiding reading for meaning, then they could use Table 5–1, which suggests techniques according to the phase of instruction (before, during, or after) that promotes meaning construction using a written response or oral discussion. Thus, the instructional technique as implemented by the teacher supports meaning construction for readers. If the area of concern is fluency, the teacher might use the matrix (Table 5–3) for skill development to select a technique by looking under the fluency column. Thus, during the strategy and skill section of the lesson framework, the teacher can increase fluency development. Use of tables in Chapter 5 facilitates instructional decision making.

1

Teachers as Problem Solvers

Teachers use instruction to understand how students read and respond to what they read. They observe learners as they read and analyze students' behaviors prompting them to use alternatives as they teach. Thus, teachers are problem solvers using instruction to provide information about learners' strengths, strategies, and needs.

The report *Preventing Reading Difficulties* states, "It is imperative that teachers at all grade levels understand . . . the role of instruction in optimizing literacy development" (Snow, Burns, & Griffin, 1998, p. 9). With knowledge about reading and reading instruction, teachers can adapt instruction to meet the strengths and needs of readers. Instruction that is tailored to their patterns of learning heightens students' engagement and enhances their ability to construct meaning when reading.

The teacher identifies specific instructional alternatives for readers to enhance their literacy. As a reader begins to experience success, she attributes her reading improvement to using strategic processes. This attribution, in turn, increases her engagement during subsequent literacy events. The teacher's task is to monitor this improvement and identify the instructional modifications that produced it. Therefore, he formulates hypotheses by observing the instructional conditions that improve reading.

> The teacher is an active problem solver. He knows a student's reading is affected not only by what she knows but also by the strategies she uses and the situation in which she reads.

The teacher is an active problem solver. He is much more than a test giver. He is first and foremost a teacher and as such, he continually explores how a particular student reads and responds. He knows that reading is affected not only by what a student knows but also by the strategies she uses and the situation in which she reads. Thinking about what the student already knows and does when he learns, the teacher selects techniques that will facilitate learning in the most efficient way. Rather than looking for causes of reading disabilities, the teacher focuses on what students can do, then coordinates their strengths with suitable reading experiences.

Active Reading

The teacher makes instructional decisions based on his understanding of how reading occurs. In this book, reading is viewed as a process that involves using both (a) information from the letters and words in the text and (b) information that the reader already knows to construct meaning within a social context. The reader is an active learner who interprets and responds to what she reads using what the text says (text-based information) and what she knows (reader-based information). The student strategically combines these information sources when reading; she also relies on both text and personal knowledge when communicating her own ideas about text within a social context. Active readers use the following processes:

1. Active readers coordinate the reading process, combining both the text and personal knowledge. While reading, such readers construct a tentative model of meaning based on inferences about the author's intended meaning. They shift between using what they know (reader-based inferencing) and what the text says (text-based inferencing) to construct their model of meaning (Duke & Pearson, 2002).

2. Active readers elaborate what and how they read (Pressley, 2000). They think about how the text they are reading relates to what they know and elaborate the strategies they are using to construct their understanding. Thus, they make connections that help them remember and interpret what they read. These new connections become part of what readers know. Likewise, readers expand their strategy options as they read and embed new strategies within their repertoire of strategies.

3. Active readers monitor their understanding to see if it makes sense (Alexander & Jetton, 2000). If it does not make sense, effective readers check their purposes for reading to see if they are on the right track, check their own knowledge and compare it to what they are reading, and vary their strategies to remove difficulties as they try to construct meaning.

4. Active readers use their knowledge and perceptions of the social context to select both their strategies and the information they use. In essence, the situation in which literacy occurs—such as a classroom group, friends talking on their way to school, or a one-to-one

tutoring session—influences what students select as important to discuss, what they elaborate, what strategies they use, and how they engage the text in order to construct meaning (Au, 2002). When their engagement seems inappropriate, they think about the literacy situation as well as past situations and ask themselves, "What response would be appropriate for this situation?"

> Reading is an active process in which readers shift between sources of information (what they know and what the text says), elaborate meaning and strategies, check their interpretation (revising when appropriate), and use the social context to focus their response.

The following scenario illustrates the process of active reading when a reader encounters an unknown word. A text has a picture of a baseball diamond with a figure running toward second base at the top of a page and the following sentence at the bottom of the page: "The girl hit the home run." From the picture of the baseball diamond, Bobby guesses that the story is about a boy. However, when he reads the sentence, the graphic cue *g* instead of *b* helps him figure out that the story is about a girl rather than a boy. Bobby's initial hypothesis, that the story is about a boy, is based on his previous experiences with similiar situations and stories.

The reader selects cues from the text and measures them against his own background knowledge and important textual information already established (*combines sources of information*). If the response is confirmed, or fits, reading continues. For example, when Bobby could not confirm the expected response in the baseball story because the word *girl* does not look like *boy,* he asked himself, "What word is like *boy* that begins with a *g*?" In other words, he wanted to know what word semantically and graphically fits (*monitors reading*).

Our experiences and the language used to describe them build our schema, or our personal worldview. Although in their own experience, children may know that both boys and girls play baseball, they may view baseball as more associated with males because of the professional games they see on TV and the many baseball books available about male stars. Because of this knowledge (*use of situational context*), Bobby in the baseball story example expected the main character to be a boy. He then revised the expected response of *boy* according to grapho-phonic information, and he read the sentence in the text as "The girl hit the home run." Reading this story caused the reader to refine the schema that "stories about baseball usually have boys for heroes" to be more specific, namely, that "stories about baseball usually have boys for heroes, but sometimes they have girls (*elaborate*)." With this experience, along with other similar experiences, Bobby began to elaborate strategies for reading and at the grading period was able to name some things good readers do when they read (*elaborate strategies*). See Figure 1–1, for example.

The model just described can provide a framework for analyzing the behaviors of problem readers. As Bobby did in the example, readers consider

Name some things good readers do when they read.

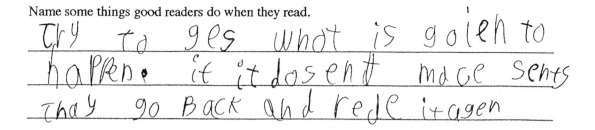

Try to ges what is golen to happen. if it dosent mace sents thay go Back and rede itagen

Figure 1–1   *Second Grade Explanation of What Good Readers Do*

many factors within any given reading event to make sense of what they are reading. Thus, all readers "draw on their prior experiences, their interactions with other readers and writers, their knowledge of word meaning and of other text, their word identification strategies, and their understanding of textual features" (*Standards for English Language Arts,* p. 3, 1996). This active process is at the heart of instructional decisions teachers make. The report *Preventing Reading Difficulties* points out that "effective reading instruction is built on a foundation that recognizes that reading outcomes are determined by complex and multifaceted factors" (Snow, Burns, & Griffin, 1998, p. 313). Therefore, the teacher examines the strategies and knowledge of problem readers in relation to active readers. Thus, a reading problem, rather than being a static deficit within the reader, is a set of strengths and weaknesses affected by interactions among many factors and instruction.

Problem Readers

Although readers use their strengths to solve problems in interpreting text, sometimes these strengths can result in compensatory behaviors that actually inhibit rather than enhance the construction of meaning. While effective readers combine sources of information, problem readers vary in their use of strategies. The point of view of this text is that problem readers often experience a deficit in either a strategy or a skill that causes them to shift away from one information source. They compensate by using their strength and thus eliminate a need to use their deficient knowledge source (Taylor et al., 1995).

This overreliance on their strength often results in inefficient reading. For example, readers who easily learn to decode words and recall text-based information often develop the idea that reading is simply repeating a string of words from the text. They become bound by the text and *do not combine both the text and their experiences.* This behavior is often coupled with the likelihood that the student will be placed in a text that is difficult for her and asked to read fewer authentic texts (Allington, 2001). Effective readers elaborate both the content and their strategies, but when reading overly challenging texts, problem readers cannot readily elaborate either the content or their strategy deployment. For example, if Bobby could not read the words *baseball or hit,* the sentence would have been difficult to read and Bobby would have allocated most of his resources to constructing meaning. In this case, Bobby's *elaboration would be restricted,* and he would not expand his content knowledge (sometimes *girls* can be baseball heroes) and his strategy use ("When the word that I said doesn't look like the text, I can think of another word that fits").

After an extended period of failing to combine sources of information or elaboration strategies, problem readers become accustomed to understanding only bits and pieces of what they are reading. They *refrain from monitoring* and passively read words without constructing meaning (Walker, 1990). For instance, if Bobby had an extended period of time reading difficult text, he might have continued to read the story miscalling *boy* for *girl,* thus misconstruing a major character in the story. Habitual passive reading fails to build an expectation that reading is a strategic process in which readers combine their resources to make sense of text. While effective readers readily monitor their understanding, problem readers passively read text without checking understanding, thus compounding their reading difficulty.

If readers continually fail to construct appropriate meaning when reading, they alter how they perceive themselves within the literacy context (Ruddell & Unrau, 1997). They attribute their continued failure to an ability (a fixed characteristic) that they do not possess rather than to lack of a strategic process that they can acquire. This attitude reinforces the belief that if they try to read, they will fail; and if they fail again, they are admitting their lack of ability. Knowing they have facilities in other academic situations, for instance, in mathematics, these problem readers reduce their effort, cease to try, and thus disengage from literacy activities. By disengaging, they can attribute failure to "not having tried" rather than to their lack of ability. Effective readers can choose among different strategies as they read, while problem readers come to *view literacy situations as self-defeating* and decrease their engagement.

> Rather than actively constructing meaning, problem readers perpetually read with one or more of the following characteristics. They (a) overrely on a single information source (usually a strength), (b) read difficult text with little or no elaboration of content and strategies, (c) read without monitoring meaning, resulting in passive reading, or (d) define reading as a failure situation and decrease their engagement.

Instructional Process

The goal of teaching is to establish appropriate learning opportunities for readers. If the students use effective strategies and make adjustments for themselves, a simple framework of active reading, and responding is sufficient.

Some readers, however, have difficulty making adjustments and employing effective strategies. Inefficient readers often need to be shown exactly how to use effective reading strategies. They need instruction that is modified during the lesson framework. The teacher, as a result, continually assesses what and how readers are learning and makes instructional adjustments to ensure successful reading. The process of adjusting instruction to ensure learning is called *mediating learning.*

> The teacher mediates learning, which means he adjusts instruction to ensure successful interpretation of text.

The teacher specifically selects activities that will directly mediate learning for each problem reader. He establishes what the student already knows and adjusts instruction to overlap her present knowledge with new information. Furthermore, he evaluates how the student learned what she knows to establish strategy strengths. Some readers rely heavily on their strengths; therefore, the teacher selects a technique that allows them to demonstrate these strengths. During instruction, the teacher discusses these strengths with students and shows them how to use these strengths in various literacy situations. As students experience success with the new reading task, the teacher selects techniques that have a more balanced instructional approach. This approach allows the teacher to use the learners' strengths (what they already know and do) to show them how to use their weaker information source when reading.

Teaching techniques were developed from different views of reading and learning. Five views are described briefly here:

- *Text-Based View.* Simply stated, this view of reading focuses on text-based processing as the major instructional concern of teachers. Learning to read is viewed as a series of associations or subskills that are reinforced until they become automatic. Letters are linked to form words, words are linked to form sentences, and sentences are linked to form ideas; that is, the parts of reading are put together to form the whole in text-based processing. Processing text shapes the learner's response.

- *Reader-Based View.* This view of reading focuses on reader-based processing as the major instructional concern of teachers. The reader is viewed as an active thinker who predicts what the author is saying. Then she samples textual information to check her predictions. Readers may actually verify their ideas about what the author is saying with a minimal amount of textual cues. Thus, reading is viewed as negotiating meaning between an author and a reader. In the reader-based view, the reader's ideas create a response.

- *Interactive View.* The interactive view of reading focuses on the active-constructive nature of reading as the major instructional concern of teachers. The reader is viewed as using both reader-based processing and text-based processing to form a model of meaning. Although she is active, her predictions are formed on the basis of what the text says and what she already knows about this information; that is, reading is viewed as constructing meaning using various information sources. Thus, reading is an interactive process in which the reader strategically shifts between the text and what she already knows to construct a response.

- *Socio-Interactive View.* This view focuses on situating understanding as a major instructional concern of teachers. As a reader discusses her response, she shifts between constructing ideas about what she personally understands and considering the ideas others have. Thus, during the discussion, she reconstructs her understanding as a result of rethinking her ideas and those of her peers. Thus, reading is viewed as a socio-interactive process in which the reader responds to text using her personal knowledge and feelings, framing and reframing her response according to the social situation.

The teaching techniques associated with differing points of view can be matched to learner strengths and needs. The teacher *chooses* techniques for reading instruction based on strengths and allows the student to read authentic literature to construct meaning. On the other hand, the teacher is cognizant of techniques that would develop the strategies and skills the learner needs to learn. The teacher's point of view for instruction is based on the classroom and student responses to instruction; however, as he plans for instruction, the teacher *balances* his instruction.

- *Balanced Instructional View.* Balanced instruction requires the thoughtful orchestration of instructional procedures. It does not require equal time for every type of activity but that the teacher view the activities as equally important. Thus, the teacher strives for *balance* in his instruction. He understands the various views of reading and "makes thoughtful choices each day about the best way to help each child become a better reader and writer" (Spiegel, 1998, p. 116). The teacher readily balances his instruction among the various views of reading, always mindful of learners' needs. He balances both text-based approaches and reader-based approaches to plan and modify his instruction. He balances supported, teacher-directed instruction with learner-centered, inquiry approaches. Likewise, he balances techniques that promote active discussion in a group of peers with settings in which the student responds on her own. The teacher uses his understanding of students, instruction, and assessment to select instructional techniques that allow students to use their strengths. Then he uses these strengths to show students how to construct meaning.

Summary

The process of teaching uses instruction to understand how readers approach the reading event. The goal of teaching is to identify instructional alternatives that create enhanced reading performance for readers. Instruction mediates learning; instruction is adjusted to ensure that readers construct meaning with text. The teacher focuses on how the learner constructs meaning by gathering data as he teaches. Furthermore, he views reading as an active process in which the reader uses what she knows to interpret what the text says within the social interactions of the literacy event. Therefore, the teacher uses the student's strengths (knowledge and strategies) to lead the student to integrate new information as well as new strategies into her reading repertoire.

2

The Roles of Effective Teachers

Effective teachers assume various roles as they teach. These roles are interrelated and provide the cornerstone of effective teaching. As he assumes these roles, he considers the variables of the reading event (task, text, reader, technique, and context), which are influences that inform instructional decision making. At the core of decision making is the effective teacher who reflects on her instruction. This chapter delineates five roles of effective teachers: reflecting, planning, mediating, enabling, and responding. These roles are supported by eight instructional guidelines that help focus teaching and encourage students to realize their individual potential as learners. As the effective teacher assumes these roles, she views readers from different perspectives. As she reflects on her decision making, therefore, she considers each of these roles and its influence on her instruction. Figure 2–1 suggests the interrelationships between the roles and guidelines discussed in this chapter.

The first role of the effective teacher is reflecting. Central to effective teaching is the teacher who reflects on teaching before, during, and after the reading event. She checks the instructional decisions she makes with her personal assumptions about reading and cross-checks her plans with students' learning. As she is teaching, she analyzes how she modifies instruction and the language she uses to mediate learning. Teaching as reflecting means that every interaction is analyzed so that appropriate instructional adjustments can be made.

The second role of the teacher is planning. As the teacher plans her lesson, she thinks about the *whole act of reading* and selects experiences for students to share their ideas. As she plans her lessons, she selects activities that will not only stimulate learning, but *ensure success*. To do so, she uses familiar and interesting stories. At the end of the lesson, the teacher encourages students to evaluate their experiences focusing their attention on their developing strengths. Teaching as planning means that the teacher focuses on the whole act of reading, ensuring success for each student.

The third role of teaching is mediating. The effective teacher *encourages active reading* on the part of learners by asking questions that not only

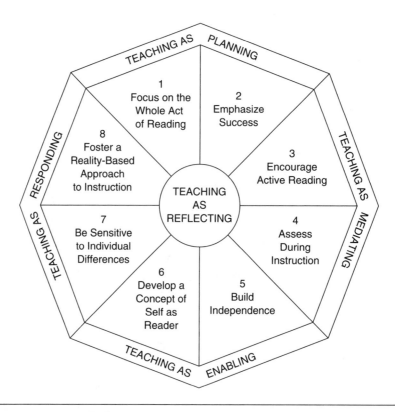

Figure 2–1 *Roles of Effective Teachers*

lead students through the story but also relate the events and key ideas to what students already know. As she teaches, the effective teacher actively aids students in sense making, phasing in to support reading and phasing out to promote self-directed learning. During the lesson, the teacher *assesses while she instructs* so she can modify her instruction to meet students' changing instructional needs. Teaching as mediating means that the teacher uses students' present strategies to lead them to more active reading strategies.

The fourth role of effective teaching is enabling. She helps her students develop a *concept of themselves as readers.* Immersing her students in relevant and successful reading experiences, she attributes their success to the effective strategies they use. As she plans lessons, she thinks about how to *build students' independence.* She plans lessons where she models her own internal thinking, asks students to share in thinking through the problem, and actively listens and encourages students to tell her how they construct meaning. Teaching as enabling means that the teacher provides students with the resources to understand themselves as readers, thinkers, and problem solvers.

In the fifth role, the teacher views teaching as responding to individual human needs. An effective teacher *accepts the individual differences* among her students. She knows that the experiences of her students vary widely and plans her instruction to account for the differences in what her students already know. She thinks about the different ways her students solve problems and plans lessons that use their problem-solving strengths. In accepting their individual differences, the effective teacher *fosters a reality-oriented environment* by accepting individuality but expecting all students to read. She uses humor and laughter to develop a relaxed atmosphere where students learn to cope with their mistakes and produce well-thought-out ideas. She also reacts personally to literacy, sharing her personal change as a result of being literate. In other words, she shares how literacy has changed her life. Teaching as a human response means that the teacher treats individuality and making mistakes as human conditions.

These roles and the instructional guidelines they represent work together to create an instructional environment where all students learn. This model fosters instructional interactions that focus on the whole reading event, giving students control of their own learning and creating a coherent learning experience for them.

Reflecting

The reflective teacher considers and selects among instructional alternatives and, at the same time, anticipates the consequences of differing decisions before, during, and after a reading event. This reflection helps teachers know why they teach as they do and facilitates their explanations to others (Roskos & Walker, 1994). The teacher shifts between immersion in the reading event and distancing herself from it in order to critically analyze the experience. This distancing helps the teacher reconsider reasons for her instruction and refocus on the theoretical framework that underpins these decisions. Thus, in reflecting, the teacher continually evaluates her guiding theory of reading (see Chapter 1) and expands her awareness of individual differences among students.

Before the lesson, the teacher plans her instruction based on her guiding theory of reading. She thinks about students' strengths and needs in relation to students' knowledge, strategies, and engagement. She reflects upon the instructional sequence as she plans each lesson. Lessons are much more than a set of activities selected because they are fun. Teaching involves the systematic orchestration of reading instruction. At this stage in the teacher's thinking (*reflections before teaching*), the students' attributes are matched with an instructional framework (see Chapter 3), and her plans are cross-checked with her guiding theory.

As the lesson is taught, the teacher observes how the student is responding to the lesson (*reflections during instruction*). Using these observations, the teacher changes original plans to modify instruction and thus to mediate student learning. Every day teachers make decisions that are often intuitive and unconscious. These changes enable readers to employ independent strategies. For example, after a fourth-grade teacher finished working with a student she reflected in this way:

> *During the lesson, I discarded the story map, modeled self-talk, self-questioning, and especially prediction. I used the story map as a summary. . . . The student elaborated and answered with background knowledge the comprehension questions today. (Jordan, 1989)*

In this example, the teacher makes adjustments during the lesson to improve the student's reading. The teacher is constantly sensitive to how the student-teacher interactions affect the goals of the lesson.

After the lesson, the teacher evaluates what specific part of the lesson produced the desired reading behavior, and she considers how the on-the-spot adjustments fit into the overall lesson. She considers the amount of energy expended in order to encourage student understanding. Likewise, she reflects on the scaffolding, or prompts, she used to improve reading performance. Then she makes adjustments in subsequent lesson plans as she reflects on what occurred and how the interactions were consistent with her plans as well as her beliefs about reading.

The reflective teacher analyzes her own preferences for learning and how these preferences affect her teaching. She focuses on how she learns and how she teaches, not only on what she is teaching. She watches herself to cross-check strategies for teaching with personal beliefs about reading. The teachers' beliefs about reading affect how they teach (Ruddell & Unrau, 1994). Reflective teachers review their assumptions about literacy.

Finally, the teacher thinks about how this instructional event brought a new understanding to her theory of reading instruction. For example, one teacher was uncertain how to measure passive reading; she had a student who was not constructing meaning but simply repeating the words in the text. After teaching, she decided to review several articles on passive behavior in reading. She later commented: "I understand that there is no testing that particularly tests this element. It is determined by observation and analysis of the reader and the reading event." After analyzing the characteristics described in the research literature, she felt she knew enough to identify one of her students as a passive reader. These reflections led the teacher to become more confident in her own knowledge. By reflecting on the various aspects of an instructional event and thinking about how they fit together, the teacher elaborates and changes her model of the reading process. Through reflection, she actively constructs her theory of reading and reading instruction.

Thus, the teacher reflects on her plans, her observations during instruction, and her intuitive decisions (adjustments). She uses these reflections as she plans lessons, mediates learning, enables student independence, and responds personally during the reading event.

■ *Planning*

Prior to the reading event, the teacher thinks about how instruction will occur. She thinks about the variables of the reading event: task, text, reader, and context. Then she selects teaching techniques that focus on reading stories that ensure student success. As teachers focus on the broad aspects of reading, they talk with students about why and how the strategies of reading will improve their reading performance. Through this interaction they create activities that are both challenging and successful.

This planning creates an expectation that the reading event will produce independent readers. Effective teachers expect the students in their classrooms to read and interpret stories. Furthermore, this planning allows the effective teacher to think about the strategies needed to complete the assigned reading task; therefore, she can attribute students' success to both their strategy use and efforts. Teaching as planning means that the teacher sets up her lessons both to focus on the whole act of reading and to ensure success. These two planning guidelines are delineated in the following section.

Guideline #1: Focus on the Whole Act of Reading

As the teacher plans her instruction, she creates a literate environment by focusing on the whole act, rather than the parts, of reading. Furthermore, she realizes that students learn what teachers teach. If teachers instruct students to recognize vowel sounds, they will learn vowel sounds. If teachers emphasize literal comprehension, students will, in fact, become excellent fact finders and comprehend the literal information of a story. However, if teachers instruct students to respond to whole stories using important textual information and their own prior knowledge, students will become comprehenders who flexibly shift between reader-based and text-based knowledge. As a result, focusing instruction on the whole act of reading is extremely important.

Effective teachers focus on having students *read entire stories* and relate them to relevant personal experiences. They encourage sustained silent reading of stories. However, studies have shown not all students receive the same amount of contextual reading instruction. A longitudinal study that investigated children's reading progress in first through third grade (Juel, 1998) found that poor readers read less than half as many words each year as good readers. Another study found that in Title I and special education programs, the amount of contextual reading was reduced rather than increased when students were placed in these special programs (Allington, 2001). Poor readers, in fact, spent an extended amount of time practicing the skills of reading in short, isolated drills (Allington, 1995). Even though research supports the premise that skill knowledge is best mastered during contextual reading, it appears that remedial instruction in both classrooms and clinics continues to focus on the parts rather than the whole act of reading. However, classrooms with high reading achievement are characterized by reading of selections followed by small-group discussions where students exchange ideas about the meaning of the story (Taylor et al., 2002). Through the small-group discussions, students justify their interpretations by relating the text to what they already know, which focuses instruction on meaning rather than decoding.

As teachers focus on the whole act of reading, they engage students in a *discussion about both the content of the story and the strategies* they use to construct meaning. This social interaction is critical to the process of constructing knowledge. As students explain and defend their ideas to their peers, they refine and reorganize their knowledge (Spiegel, 1998). Likewise, students who hold misconceptions about the content need to be challenged by others to redefine their understanding and create new knowledge. By communicating ideas in discussion groups, students share their interpretations, focus their purposes, and think about the functions of reading and writing. The teacher plans time for discussing stories in both small-group and large-group settings so that students can explore their own interpretation with classmates.

The teacher plans for the *engagement of all students* in an instructional group. Research shows that remedial instruction focusing on individualization means that each child "will work, primarily alone, on a different skill sheet. . . . Each child receives but a few moments of teacher attention" (Johnston & Allington, 1991, p. 994). Realizing that learning is a social activity, the teacher makes sure all students interact in discussion groups, sharing their ideas about stories they have read. Therefore, as she plans for student engagement, she reminds herself of the social nature of literacy development and thus encourages active engagement in literacy for all students in her classroom.

In summary, the effective teacher encourages students to discuss ideas during the reading event. She explains the process of shifting between reader-based knowledge and the text and how the strategies of reading will influence reading efficiency when problems in text interpretation arise. The teacher carefully orchestrates these discussions to engage all students.

GUIDELINE #1: FOCUS ON THE WHOLE ACT OF READING

- Focus on reading entire stories.
- Plan time for discussing content and strategies.
- Plan for the engagement of all students.

Guideline #2: Emphasize Success

As the teacher focuses on the whole act of reading, she must at the same time ensure successful reading for students. Students' reading achievement is directly related to their engagement in successful literacy activities. In addition to the amount of time engaged in reading, a high level of success is also crucial. Thus in order to develop a notion of efficient reading, students must first experience numerous successful reading experiences. When students have success, they tend to repeat the successful activity. Obviously, success is a powerful motivating factor.

On the other hand, if students experience numerous failures in an activity, they often give up and avoid subsequent opportunities to engage in this activity. Poor readers often read material that is difficult for them (Allington, 2001). They have a low rate of either recognizing words or understanding the content, which discourages them from further reading. These unsuccessful reading experiences contribute to an unsystematic evaluation of reading performance. These students have a serendipitous notion about success. Success is attributed to external factors such as "It was baby reading material," "It was my lucky day," or "The teacher gave it away when she helped me."

To encourage a healthy attitude toward success, the teacher creates a *series of consistently successful reading events*. She keeps a close match between the students' abilities and the texts that she chooses for reading instruction. When choosing texts, the teacher considers not only an appropriate difficulty level but also the extent of students' prior experiences. She chooses material that contains familiar concepts so that students can readily use their prior knowledge to predict, monitor, and elaborate their understanding. She then plans for the students to read a greater amount of material and to express ideas based on what they have read.

Not only does the diagnostic teacher plan successful reading experiences by placing the students at the appropriate reading level, but she also carefully selects *authentic texts that are familiar and interesting* to her students. Good children's literature presents characters who share similar experiences with readers, thus promoting students' ability to read for meaning. When children's literature is matched with students' experiences, the problem readers readily identify with the main character's conflict and can successfully predict solutions out of their own experiences. Therefore, the teacher selects high-caliber children's literature and reads with students to establish a successful reading experience. The students can continue to read on their own and feel the success of reading an entire book. This success can spill over into other literacy activities by giving students confidence in writing or in taking on other reading tasks.

However, many problem readers have a hazy notion of success and do not recognize when they are successful. Therefore, besides creating successful experiences, the teacher designs activities that concretely show students how they are progressing. The teacher *encourages self-assessment,* which helps readers evaluate and recognize their success. Portfolios, in which students choose what is included in their assessment folder, can help them evaluate their success on various activities and show them their progress over time. Periodically, the teacher uses these portfolios to show students their growth in strategic reading and knowledge acquisition. Students can also evaluate their success on individual reading activities as they complete them by using teacher-developed check-sheets related to the task. For example, a check-sheet was designed with story grammar questions (see "Story Mapping," Part Two). The students marked whether their retelling included main characters, setting, problem, major events, and problem resolution. Using the check-sheet, the students and teacher assess literacy and discuss student success. Self-assessment helps problem readers develop a more systematic evaluation of reading performance and attribute their success to internal factors such as knowledge and strategies rather than to luck or easy materials.

GUIDELINE #2: EMPHASIZE SUCCESS

- Create a series of successful reading events.
- Use authentic texts that are familiar and interesting.
- Encourage self-assessment.

Mediating

The teacher mediates learning by phasing in and out of the reading event as she adjusts her instruction to students' needs. She asks questions that help students actively interpret the text. She listens to the students and uses what they understand about the story to elicit more elaborate interpretations. She gives them time to develop predictions and formulate answers. When students are unsure of a response, she asks them what they know so far about the story. Then she asks them to explain how they came to that conclusion. From this information, the teacher develops leading questions or examples that will guide students' interpretations. Using students' responses, the teacher assesses their learning as she teaches. Teaching as mediating means that the teacher phases in and out of the reading event both to encourage active reading and to assess learning as she teaches. These two mediating guidelines are detailed in the following section.

Guideline #3: Encourage Active Reading

Reading is an active, problem-solving process that involves predicting (or guessing) what the author is going to say, based on expectations about story events. After making a guess, students select clues from the story to confirm their guesses and then check this knowledge with what they already know. The teacher engages students in this active problem-solving process so they construct meaning as they read. This engagement fosters students' exploration of their own concepts and strategies. From a young age, children strive to make sense of their world, and the teacher builds on this natural aptitude by supporting students in *making sense of reading and writing events*. The teacher encourages students to evaluate their guesses from a sense-making perspective. She assists students to extend ideas, revise misconceptions, develop opinions, and prove beliefs. In their search for meaning, students invent their own explanations for print, examine and justify these hypotheses, and finally refute or rework their explanations. To mediate learning, the teacher constantly engages students in an active meaning search.

To do so, the teacher checks her behavior with both proficient and problem readers to see whether her prompts focus on meaning. Research shows that teachers treat their less proficient readers differently from their proficient readers (Allington, 2001). When working with proficient readers, teachers are more engaged using meaning-level prompts and letting good readers continue reading to see whether they are going to recover meaning. However, when working with less proficient readers, teachers often allow more interruptions, interrupt poor readers at the point of error, and use more word-level prompting before correcting them. These teaching behaviors often cause poor readers to miscall words or ideas and continue reading without checking these words or ideas against an overall meaning to see whether they fit. For these readers, the teacher needs to frame her prompts from a sense-making perspective. As students miscall a word or miscomprehend an idea, she indicates her inability to make sense of their response and encourages them to rethink their explanation. This approach focuses the problem reader on making sense of text. For example, the teacher might say the following:

What would make sense and start with an "s"?

Think about the story; what would make sense, and start with the sound "s-s-s"?

Look at the picture; what would make sense, and fit with the picture?

The teacher combines these responses in a variety of ways to help the reader focus on making sense of text.

As the teacher responds to the discussion, she thinks about how to orchestrate her support. The effective teacher *phases in to support the students' sense making and phases out to allow students to think independently.* Initially, she allows 3 to 5 seconds between her probes and the student's response. Increasing the wait time from 1 second to 3 seconds positively affects the number of student responses as well as the organization of the response (Allington & Cunningham, 2002). Furthermore, the amount of time between the students' responses and the teacher's response affects the elaboration of the answer. Thinking takes time. Silence may mean that students are constructing thoughtful responses.

Not only should the teacher increase her wait time, but she must also deal effectively with inappropriate responses. Initially, the teacher uses part of the student's response to probe reasoning. Sometimes she rephrases or repeats part of the student's response to clarify the interpretations. At other times, she asks students to justify their answers by supplying information from the text. She probes student reasoning by asking "How do you know that?" and "What makes you think that?" Finally, if the line of reasoning is justifiable, the teacher accepts the response as a valid point of view. As the teacher increases her wait time and deals creatively with inappropriate responses, she develops an atmosphere that promotes active interpretation of text.

The teacher can encourage active reading by *creating instructional conversations* (Goldenberg, 1992–1993) and focusing on constructing ideas rather than giving right or wrong answers. The teacher creates a shared activity in which the students and teacher can discuss their ideas rather than the traditional recitation format used in classrooms. As they discuss ideas, the teacher connects the students' statements, helping students build a cohesive understanding. She interjects open-ended comments that encourage rethinking of ideas, and she invites students to expand their thinking by saying "tell me more," encouraging them to connect important ideas in the text with their own knowledge.

In summary, the teacher encourages active reading by focusing students on making sense of text and probing student responses in order to support their active reflection. She phases in and out of the lesson to create an atmosphere that promotes thinking rather than interrogation. To increase students' understanding, she engages students in conversations about text where they elaborate their thinking.

GUIDELINE #3: ENCOURAGE ACTIVE READING

- Focus on sense making with text.
- Phase in and out to support active thinking.
- Create conversations about the text.

Guideline #4: Assess During Instruction

As the teacher implements the lessons she planned, she keeps a mental log of the students' responses. Her instruction, therefore, not only creates active readers but also provides a means for assessment. As the teacher mediates learning, she observes how she modifies the initial reading task to create learning. In other words, she *assesses changes in the readers' performances occurring as she mediates learning.* This record of students' responses to instructional modifications is called *dynamic assessment.* Dynamic assessment evaluates students' performances as they are guided to use more effective reading strategies. This type of assessment focuses on the students' acquisition of strategies during instruction rather than unaided levels of competence.

During dynamic assessment, the teacher *probes responses.* For example, when a student read a story about two mountain climbers in Chile, South America, he miscalled the word *Chile* (actually he pronounced the *ch* sound and then mumbled). In the oral retelling, he referred to Chile as the location. When the teacher probed how he knew the country was Chile, the student said, "Well, the author talked about the Andes Mountains, and I know the Andes Mountains are on the west coast of South America . . . so I decided that the country must have been Chile."

From this information, the teacher assessed that this student had a wide range of prior knowledge and used them to interpret text. He was also able to mentally self-correct word recognition errors. This sign told her that he was an active rather than a passive reader. His reading concern stemmed from overrelying on his background knowledge when he encountered several words that he could not recognize. Probing the student about how he arrived at a response gave the teacher a more accurate picture of the student's potential for learning new information.

Finally, as the teacher assesses learning while she teaches, she evaluates whether her instruction is appropriate for her learners. She evaluates the reading event and *asks whether there is another way* to interact with the students. She asks herself:

1. Am I leading students through the task according to their present strategy use? If not, should I try another way?

2. Is this text appropriate for these students? If not, should I try another text?

3. Am I using the students' strengths as I am teaching? If not, should I try another way?

4. Is this technique appropriate for these students? If not, should I try another way?

5. Is this learning context appropriate for these students? If not, should I try another situation?

As key variables of instruction are changed, assessment is based on the resulting changes in reading performance. The teacher evaluates students' improvement as a result of her instruction. If students do not improve, the teacher looks for another way to modify instruction to enhance literacy.

GUIDELINE #4: ASSESS DURING INSTRUCTION

- Assess reading change as a result of mediated learning.
- Probe students' responses to understand their thinking.
- If reading behavior does not change, try another adjustment.

Enabling

During the reading event, the teacher enables students to be independent learners and therefore think of themselves as readers. To enable students, the teacher helps them develop independence by sharing how she thinks while she is reading. The students and teacher work together to figure out a story and then discuss how they reached their conclusions. As the teacher shares her thinking and works with the students, she enables them to control their own learning and talk through their own understanding of a story. To build students' independence, she finds ways to show them that they can read and think. She acknowledges the effective strategies they use when they read efficiently. At times, she allows students to read for their own purposes without teacher questions and discussion. These guidelines for enabling students are elaborated in the following section.

Guideline #5: Build Independence

The fifth guideline requires that the teacher both instruct the strategies of reading and systematically plan how students will assume responsibility for their own learning. Not only does the teacher direct the learning process by explaining the steps and guiding the practice, but she also gives students ownership of their learning by encouraging them to think about their thinking. Efficient readers monitor their understanding. As they are reading, they actively choose alternate strategies when the words do not make sense. Poor readers, on the other hand, are characterized by disorganized strategies and failing to self-monitor spontaneously. Consequently, they continue to rely on the teacher to monitor reading performance.

Passive readers, therefore, need instruction in effective monitoring behaviors so that they can move from teacher-directed to self-directed learning. The initial step is to redirect assessment from the teacher to the student, with the teacher demonstrating how to self-monitor reading. To do so, the teacher purposely makes mistakes while reading so that she can *demonstrate* how she monitors an active meaning search. Too often poor readers perceive proficient reading as error-free reading. By making mistakes, the teacher can demonstrate her own coping behaviors.

The teacher begins by saying, "Oops, that didn't make sense." Then she demonstrates alternative strategies. She shows readers that they can ignore the mistake and read on to see whether they can figure out the meaning, or that they can reread the sentence to check the overall meaning to see what might fit.

As she continues to demonstrate this active meaning search, the teacher illustrates the self-questioning process that goes through the mind of an active reader:

> *If I don't understand, I ask myself a series of questions, the first one being "What would make sense?" If I can't regain the meaning, I ask more questions. Most of the time I need to figure out either a word I don't know or what the author was trying to say. I can use two different sequences.*
>
> *First, to figure out a word, I ask myself, "Can I say it that way?" (syntactic fit) or "What word does it look like?" (graphic fit) or "What does it sound like?" (phonic fit).*
>
> *Second, to figure out meaning, I ask myself, "What does the text say? What do I already know about what the text says? How does this information fit together?"*

After modeling the self-questioning process, the teacher and students work through a couple of examples. The students follow the teacher's model and

I like this because, I could write what I was thinking. This shows that you can get off track & stay on track. Self-talk helps me think of what I am thinking while I read

---

Figure 2–2 *Portfolio Reflection on Self-Talk*

think aloud, asking themselves questions about their reading. The students actually talk about how they solve the reading task. As the students talk aloud, the teacher *supports their thinking by giving them hints and encouraging them to talk through their thinking*. As the students talk aloud, the teacher names the strategies that they are using. She comments, "Did you notice how you reread that sentence to see whether it made sense? That was very effective." One student reflected on her self-talk when she wrote her portfolio reflection, as shown in Figure 2–2.

As processes are demonstrated and practiced, the teacher explains when it is most appropriate to use them. For example, for different types of text, the teacher explains why or why not to use the particular reading strategy she is teaching. If the teacher is demonstrating how to formulate predictions based on prior knowledge, she explains that if the student does not know anything about the topic, he must read two or three paragraphs, summarize the information, and then create a prediction based on the just-learned information. Teacher and student thus *collaborate in thinking* about various ways strategic reading changes in different situations.

The teacher builds student independence by demonstrating the process of active reading and the corresponding troubleshooting strategies that efficient readers use. In addition, the teacher thinks out loud, showing students how she knows what she knows. In turn, students think out loud using the steps of active reading, and the teacher supports their thinking process rather than focusing on right or wrong answers. Finally, the teacher and students collaboratively discuss how they use strategic reading in various situations.

GUIDELINE #5: BUILD INDEPENDENCE

- Demonstrate thinking.
- Support thinking by encouraging self-talk.
- Collaborate in thinking about when to use strategies.

Guideline #6: Develop a Concept of Self as Reader

Children come to school with well-developed problem-solving abilities; they have learned to walk, to talk, and so on. Through their everyday living, they have learned many of the principles of communicating their ideas through language. However, because problem readers repeatedly fail when learning to read, they develop a concept of themselves as nonreaders. This self-assessment is difficult to change. As inefficient readers learn to read, word identification is often difficult for them, and the sympathetic teacher assists these students more readily, allowing them to depend on teacher assistance. This type of interaction inhibits learners' active search for meaning and encourages a passive view of reading.

While listening to such readers, an effective teacher notices that they read as if they do not expect the text to make sense. They read as if they believe getting every word right is reading (Goodman, 1996). This passive attitude is also exhibited when comprehending text. These readers seem to monitor their reading less frequently and accept whatever argument is presented in the text without applying their prior knowledge. They seldom reread text to check initial interpretations and try to maintain interpretations even in light of contradictory information (Paris, Lipson, & Wixson, 1994). These ineffective strategies can be altered by the teacher who is sensitive to her influence on the students' concept of themselves as readers. This concept can be developed using three teaching strategies: immersing students in reading, attributing success to effective strategy use, and allowing time for personal reading.

To be engaged in the actual reading of text is the first important prerequisite for developing a concept of self as reader. *Immersing students in relevant reading activities* will increase their concept of themselves as readers. As students read material that is relevant, repetitive, and rhythmic, they can feel themselves reading. Poor readers, however, have few opportunities to read connected text. In first-grade classrooms, Allington (2001) reports that children in high reading groups read three times as many words as children in low reading groups. Therefore, increasing the amount of fluent contextual reading students engage in each day is the first step toward helping them develop a concept of self as reader. Difficult reading material causes students to focus on the word level of reading, precluding an active search for meaning. Reading text fluently at an *easy reading level* allows students to read enough words correctly so that they can engage in an active search for meaning.

Inefficient readers, however, need more than easy reading material to change their concept of themselves as readers. As the children build their self-concepts as readers, a second major task of the teacher is to talk about the strategies used to derive meaning from text and *attribute active reading to effective strategy use and effort* (Schunk & Zimmerman, 1997). Because of the repeated failures of problem readers, they do not recognize the effective strategies they do use. When asked how they got an answer, students often respond with "I don't know." These students do not have enough experience with successful reading to recognize when and how their effective strategies work. Often, they attribute their reading performance to forces outside their control rather than to effective use of strategies. To change this attitude, teachers show students how their strategies influence reading performance. As students engage in reading, the teacher points out or names the strategy they are using. The teacher follows this up by attributing success to effective strategy use and effort. Using self-assessment charts (see Chapter 3), the students' attention is refocused on those behaviors they can control. When effective strategies are supported, students can attribute their comprehension not only to the product but also to the process of active reading. They begin to see themselves as active readers who can construct meaning from text.

The purpose for reading can also influence students' concepts of themselves as readers. When students read for their own purposes and enjoyment, their interactions with text are perceived as real and relevant reading; consequently, they perceive themselves as readers. Teachers need to set aside time in the classroom for children to *read for their own purposes* and then share their reading. In building the students' concept of themselves as readers, the teacher allows time for them to share the knowledge they have gained from reading in a creative way with their peers. She creates a "read and tell" time that reinforces individual variation in text interpretation. This activity allows students to have ownership of their own responses to the text and builds the concept of themselves as readers.

When students think of themselves as readers, they actively engage in text interpretation. They view themselves as in control of their reading. The sensitive teacher creates independent readers by having them read a lot of text, stressing the strategies of active reading, and having them read relevant materials for their own purposes.

GUIDELINE #6: DEVELOP A CONCEPT OF SELF AS READER

- Immerse students in reading.
- Help students attribute active reading to effective strategy use.
- Allow students to read and write for their own individual purposes.

Responding

In all her interactions, the teacher responds as a person. She responds to the different students in her classroom and challenges them according to their individual needs. She uses what they already know to present concepts in the way they learn best. Using the unique strengths of the individual learners in her classroom, she reduces stress for each learner. Furthermore, she acknowledges the realities of the educational situation. Using personal statements about her own reading process and laughing about her own mistakes increase students' awareness that reading is constructing a response rather than getting the answer right.

Guideline #7: Be Sensitive to Individual Differences

Students bring to the reading task their own sets of experiences and knowledge, which affect their reading behavior. At the same time, they bring their own strategies for dealing with the world. Some children are impulsive, some are extremely verbal, and some are quiet. Even though each of them is different, seldom do these differences affect instruction in public schools, partly because the exploration of how learners are alike and different is limited. Understanding human similarities can increase one's sensitivity to human differences.

People learn new information in two ways. First, they all use what they already know to formulate hypotheses about new information. Second, they use their strengths to reduce this stress (learn the information). Therefore, in this state of disequilibrium (new learning), people use what they already know to make sense of the new information. However, people differ not only on *what* they already know (knowledge-based differences) but also on *how* they integrate new information with what they already know (strategy-based differences).

Knowledge-based differences are evident in the scope of vocabulary knowledge and the variety of experiences that students have. Some children come to school with a rich variety of experiences and well-developed oral language. Some children have had repeated experiences with books and have developed concepts about print. Other children come to school with limited experiences with reading events and require more exposure to a variety of experiences with both print and concepts.

These knowledge-based differences are accentuated by differences in problem-solving strategies. All students do not learn the same way. Some students select meaning cues, while others select graphic cues. For example, Clay (1993) found that many young readers did not integrate cueing systems. Some of these students used a visual cueing system; they matched the missed word with the initial letters of other words they knew. Other students used the phonic cueing system; they matched the missed word to the sounds they knew.

Some students rely heavily on their background knowledge to form hypotheses while they are reading. These students check what they already know without thinking about the text. Other students rely heavily on the text to form their hypotheses while reading (Taylor et al., 1995). Some students summarize stories, giving the overall gist of the text, while other students give explicitly stated information. Some students revise and monitor their model of meaning readily, while others need concrete facts before they revise their model of meaning. Some students organize information within broad, overlapping categories, while others organize information in discrete, hierarchical categories. Being sensitive to individual differences, the teacher *adjusts instruction, incorporating not only what students already know but also what they can do.*

The teacher thinks carefully about the individual students in her classroom. Because the reading event is more stressful for remedial readers, the demand for instruction using background knowledge and processing strengths is greater for them. The teacher *reduces stress by using students' strengths.* By using appropriate instructional methods, the teacher can reduce the stress and increase learning. For example, teachers have differentiated prompting by using language that emphasizes the preferred cueing system and then encouraging the integration of other cueing systems (Clay, 1993). For instance, the student using the visual cueing system can be prompted to use meaning-based and phonics cues by asking "What makes sense?" or "What begins with the letter . . . and makes sense in the sentence?" Teacher prompting can effectively focus instruction on using students' processing strengths and then encouraging them to incorporate more flexible strategies.

Furthermore, *individual sense making is encouraged through the use of* I *statements.* The teacher models "I think . . . ," talking about her own reading and thinking aloud about how she figured out a particular answer. Showing the *how* and modeling "I think . . . " releases students from the necessity of having to do the process in the same way. "I do it this way" implies that others can do it a different way. Furthermore, this attitude eases the need to conform and acknowledges that even though a particular process or strategy for solving problems is not an effective strategy for reading, it may be effective in other situations. For the impulsive child, the teacher often remarks, "Someday your rapid-fire decision making may help you become a great artist, but when you are reading text, you need to think about what the author is trying to say."

Being sensitive to individual differences requires that the teacher evaluate two broad categories of learner differences. First, she evaluates what students already know, because using what they already know will increase what is learned. Second, she assesses the way students learned what they already know so that new information can be presented using their strengths. These two categories, knowledge-based differences and strategy-based differences, help the teacher adjust instruction for individual students. As the teacher learns to meet the needs of her students, she uses their strengths and models *I* statements (which release everyone from doing things in the same way). Thus she encourages individual variation in problem solving.

GUIDELINE #7: BE SENSITIVE TO INDIVIDUAL DIFFERENCES

- Adjust instruction to what students already know and do.
- Reduce stress by using students' strengths.
- Use *I* statements to acknowledge individual variation in problem solving.

Guideline #8: Foster a Reality-Based Approach to Instruction

Even though each child is different and some are harder to teach than others, the teacher interacts with each of her students as a person. She is a participant in the learning process, sharing with them her reactions to reading events and student learning. Honest communication and sharing of the knowledge of the students' reading strategies sets the stage.

The teacher helps students develop a realistic assessment of their own reading behavior, as opposed to a tense, perfectionist view of their learning. Continually she demonstrates that *real life requires coping with mistakes.* She becomes human as she talks about her own mistakes and coping behaviors, focusing on the process rather than the products of reading. As the teacher finds humor in her mistakes and proceeds to correct them, so too will her students learn to reflect on their mistakes in a lighthearted manner, realizing that they can correct incongruencies as they read. Mistakes become a tool for learning rather than an indication of failure. Modeling self-correcting strategies in a relaxed atmosphere helps students develop a risk-taking attitude toward reading (Goodman & Marek, 1996) and increases their active reading behavior.

Likewise, effective teachers expect students to think, cope with their mistakes, and resolve problems as they read. As such teachers adjust instruction, they *maintain high expectations* (Taylor et al., 2002). They expect students to read lots of words and to express ideas based on what they have read. A major characteristic contributing to the success of all readers is the teacher's expectation that all students will read and learn. Maintaining appropriate expectations is extremely demanding for the teacher. It is important, however, to maintain high expectations and to share with students how those expectations are to be met. Once the teacher has made adjustments during instruction, she tells students she expects them to complete the necessary reading. She emphasizes that real life involves coping with limitations and using one's strengths to solve difficult problems.

Finally, the teacher engages students by personally responding to literature, *discussing her own personal change as a result of reading and writing experiences.* This personal response draws students into discussing their own individual reactions to literature. Consequently, both the students and the teacher talk about how their worldview is changing as a result of being literate. In this way, she fosters reality-based instruction that gives students more than a reading experience; it provides a model for how literacy stimulates people to expand their own knowledge.

In her classroom, the effective teacher creates a relaxed environment where students can take risks and correct mistakes as they try out new ideas. She expects that all students will grow and learn from their mistakes. She interacts with her students personally, sharing with them her own interpretations and growth. Thus, a reality-based approach to instruction is just that: It makes reading a real, personal event.

GUIDELINE #8: FOSTER A REALITY-BASED APPROACH TO INSTRUCTION

- Teach that real life requires coping with mistakes.
- Maintain high expectations.
- Discuss personal change as a result of reading.

Summary

Effective teaching is coordinated by the reflective teacher who bases her decision making on individual assessment of the readers' responses during instruction. Thus, at the core of teaching is reflective teaching. The effective teacher plans instruction, mediates learning, enables thinking, and responds honestly so that students experience success when reading interesting stories that require personal interpretation. Consequently, teaching requires planning a whole reading event, the emphasis of which is success. Furthermore, the teacher's goal is to create active, engaged readers who use what they already know to interpret text.

With this goal in mind, she encourages active reading by assessing reader response while she teaches. She is sensitive to the individual differences among her students and accepts the uniqueness of each reader in her classroom. She enables students to read with confidence, creating the expectation in students that they can read. She reacts to the instructional event not only as the planner, mediator, and enabler, but also as a participant in the reading event. She acknowledges her own personal response to literature and fosters in her classroom real responses to reading and thoughtful sharing of responses.

3

A Framework for Teaching Reading

A teaching framework places a premium on tailoring programs that specifically fit readers.* It provides a structure for lesson planning that uses the processes of assessment and instruction to identify instructional alternatives. The session is composed of the following four elements: (1) familiar text time, (2) guided contextual reading, (3) strategy and skill instruction, and (4) personalized reading and writing.

Each of the four elements has specific purposes within the teaching framework. *Familiar text time* provides a time for students to flexibly use their reading strategies and skills while reading easy material. It provides a balance between easy reading and the challenging tasks that lie ahead (Roskos & Walker, 1994). *Guided contextual reading* focuses on meaningful interpretation of whole stories, while allowing students to demonstrate their strengths. It involves the planning and mediating roles of the effective teacher. *Strategy and skill instruction* focuses on specific areas of concerns that might be inhibiting students' active reading. By engaging in strategy instruction, the teacher promotes student independence. During *personalized reading and writing*, both the students and the teacher engage in reading and writing for their own purposes and self-fulfillment. This element helps students develop concepts of themselves as successful readers. The students define their own goals during this element. This chapter explains the instructional premises of using a teaching framework and its features.

---

*This teaching framework is based on a teaching procedure developed by Darrel D. Ray and used in the Oklahoma State University Reading Clinic. The author is grateful for the perceptive insights gleaned from her work in that clinic.

Premises

In addition to the teacher's roles described in the previous chapter, the teaching framework is based on concepts related to *balanced* reading instruction.

1. Effective teaching results in a *balance* of contextual reading with strategy and skill instruction. Guided contextual reading uses whole stories to teach reading as students interpret and discuss text. Strategy and skill instruction provides minilessons in specific strategies or skills that are inhibiting a student's active reading.

2. Effective teaching results from monitoring the effect that instructional adjustments have on reading performance. The teacher *balances* assessment and instruction.

3. Effective teaching results from a *balance* of guided (implicit) instruction and direct (explicit) instruction. Personalized reading and writing is characterized by implicit instruction. Strategy and skill instruction, on the other hand, is characterized by minilessons that explicitly demonstrate needed strategies and skills.

4. Effective teaching is supported by a *balance* between text selected by the student and text selected by the teacher. In familiar text time and personalized reading and writing, students select the texts. In guided contextual reading and strategy and skill instruction, the teacher usually selects texts with student input.

5. Effective teaching allows students to demonstrate their strengths (what they already know and do) by overlapping what is known and done with new information and new strategies. In other words, the teacher *balances* instruction using the students' strengths with instruction in new ideas and strategies.

6. Effective teaching results from a *balance* of challenging and easy reading tasks. Guided contextual reading provides instruction in material that is moderately difficult for the student, while personalized reading and writing are characterized by easy reading material. The teacher uses a combination of moderately difficult texts and easy texts.

These premises underlie the elements of the teaching framework. Taken together, the elements provide a vehicle for monitoring the effect of instructional adjustments and the *balance* of instruction using strengths and instruction in new ideas and strategies, of contextual reading and strategy lessons, of implicit and explicit instruction, of challenging and familiar reading tasks, of self-selected materials and teacher-selected materials, and of assessment and instruction.

Familiar Text Time (FTT)

Familiar text time (FTT) is the rereading of books and poems that the student enjoys. These easy and often predictable books are authentic children's literature that can be read repeatedly because of the rhyme, rhythm, and repetition. Like singing a favorite song over and over again, this procedure engages readers in active reading and sets a supportive tone for the entire session.

During FTT the teacher invites the reader to choose among four or five familiar stories. Allowing the reader to choose what she will read increases engagement. By choosing, the reader establishes a reason for reading the selected text. She might think, "I like how the bird scares the spider so I will choose this one." Thus, the student is in control.

Familiar text also increases the amount of easy reading that the student accomplishes, which establishes a balance between easy and challenging tasks. During FTT, students use their developing strategies and skills within the context of already known material. As they try out and refine their new strategies and skills while immersed in known information, readers concentrate on implementing the new processes. The interaction between the teacher, the student, and the text provides a safety net for making and correcting mistakes, which in turn increases the active engagement of readers. They enjoy the risk-taking activity that begins instruction and continue the rest of the session with this same attitude.

FOCUS OF FAMILIAR TEXT TIME

- Refining strategies and skills.
- Reading easy, familiar material.
- Promoting high engagement.

Guided Contextual Reading (GCR)

Each teaching session includes a guided contextual reading lesson (GCR), which focuses instruction on the communication of ideas gleaned from reading whole stories. Therefore, the focus of this element is constructing meaning with text. The teacher thinks about the kind of instruction needed before, during, and after the student reads the selected story or chapter. He considers the support needed before the story to enable the student to construct meaning with text. The teacher asks himself, "Can I provide support before reading to help the student anticipate the meaning?" Then the student's attention is focused on the key concepts of the story prior to reading. These concepts are related to the student's own experience. Together teacher and student develop predictions related to the story theme, thus increasing the student's active reading of the story. Open-ended questions need to focus on predictions that will engage the student in active reading through the entire length of the story. Therefore, purposes or predictions that can be answered on the first page of the story hardly represent the main story theme.

During this brief discussion, the teacher anticipates problem vocabulary words and, if needed, provides instruction in either word identification or word meaning. This instruction needs to be directly related to the story to be read, predictions that have been made, and the key concepts or story theme. Time is of the essence in teaching. Consequently, only the important words, meanings, and concepts need to be stressed.

The second step of guided contextual reading occurs while students are reading and includes silent reading to construct meaning. The teacher thinks about what kind of support is needed as the students read the story or chapter. While discussing the story, the teacher needs to elicit responses from students that focus on the main theme. Rather than focusing on responses and questions that are text-based, literal, and unrelated to the story theme, the teacher can use questions and lead discussions that focus students on understanding the purposeful actions of the characters to resolve the problems in the story. In other words, a thematic focus and logical questions help students summarize the main actions and themes that occur in the story.

After the text is read, students respond to the passage as a whole. This requires students to analyze the story in terms of the characters' motivations, the author's purpose for writing the story, and other stories and experiences with similar themes. A key component of this phase is students relating the story to similar personal experiences and analyzing the effect these experiences have on comprehending the story. Experiences may include other stories, movies, songs that the students have encountered with similar plots and characters, as well as personal experiences. Students should focus on the similarities and differences among these cases, using textual and nontextual information to support statements.

These aspects form the instructional focus for guided contextual reading, the major component of this framework. Basic to the development of guided contextual reading is an instructional sequence that uses the students' strengths; therefore, techniques are selected so that the reader can construct meaning. In other words, the teacher asks, "What can I do to make these stories more understandable for my students? Do I need specific reading techniques to ensure active reading of these stories? At what point in the instructional sequence do I need to adjust my instruction?"

For example, students who have a limited ability to deal with oral language could receive vocabulary development and direct experiences with the prerequisite concepts that are necessary to read a particular selection with understanding. For these students, GCR requires an increased amount of instruction before they read the story. Webs (see "Webbing" in Part Two), which require students and teacher to construct a visual diagram relating the vocabulary words to background knowledge, are used to introduce the story. In this case, the instructional adjustment occurs prior to reading the story. This approach facilitates the students' understanding of the concepts in the story and increases their ability to construct meaning.

When students experience little difficulty with understanding what the words mean, however, the instructional adjustments are different. For students who show extreme difficulty with print processing, the teacher spends more time on word identification and less time on developing word meanings. Before a story is read, for example, a language experience story (see "Language Experience" in Part Two) might be written using the targeted vocabulary words. The teacher encourages rereading of this story so that the students encounter the vocabulary in text. After the selected story is read, readers theater scripts (see "Readers Theater" in Part Two) could be constructed from the story so that increasing oral reading fluency becomes purposeful. The teacher incorporates techniques both before and after the students read the story. The adjustments facilitate their ability to construct meaning with text. During GCR, the teacher differentiates instruction according to learner strengths. The ultimate goal is to focus on the whole act of reading in connected text that will allow students to integrate their prior knowledge with the text and to develop personal interpretations.

FOCUS OF GUIDED CONTEXTUAL READING

- Focus on meaning.
- Have the students read whole stories.
- Support active reading before, during, and after the lesson.
- Differentiate instruction so that the reader can construct meaning.
- Encourage personal interpretations.

Strategy and Skill Instruction (SAS)

Strategy and skill instruction (SAS) consists of a series of minilessons planned to develop and modify reading strategies. As such, the teacher selects texts to teach a designated strategy or skill. He carefully selects varying levels of text difficulty to provide for an interplay of easy and challenging reading. The basis for the effective execution of strategy and skill instruction are as follows. First, the teacher identifies those strategies and skills inhibiting proficient reading. Then lessons that explicitly teach those strategies are developed. Finally, the targeted task is monitored by the students and teacher, using a graphic representation of progress that calls for self-assessment.

Strategy and Skill Instruction

After the teacher has identified those strategies and skills inhibiting proficient reading, he creates lessons that teach those strategies. For most minilessons, the teacher selects an easy text to introduce the targeted strategy or skill, which limits other possible problems in text interpretation. As the task is learned, the teacher increases the difficulty level of the text so as to lead students to use the targeted strategy or skill in reading situations that are moderately difficult. The activities need to be carefully chosen so that the teacher can model active reading. For example, Mary, who does not use what the word looks like, or means to correct miscues, could use an adapted repeated reading (see Modification #2 in "Repeated Readings" in Part Two) that incorporates strategy instruction of the self-talk "What would make sense and starts with a . . . ?" as an intervention between the first and second readings.

Initially, students are informed of their inefficient strategies and shown the efficient counterpart. After stating how the strategy or skill works, the teacher gives students a rationale for its inclusion in their program and tells them why doing these specific activities will increase strategic reading. Then students are led systematically through a series of short activities. In the first examples, the teacher demonstrates the active reading process. Then students use the teacher's example to modify their previous strategy use.

In Mary's case, after the first reading of a selection, the teacher reviews miscues and suggests that reading would be more effective if Mary would check the miscue to see whether it made sense. Then he explains how he would self-correct those miscues using a sense-making framework and checking the initial letter of a word. For example, before the second reading, the teacher explains that when reading breaks down, Mary should ask what would make sense and starts with the same letter as the word in the text. "If I had made this mistake," says the teacher, "I would have asked, 'What would Dad use that starts with a *sh*?' Then I would have corrected the sentence to read 'Dad shoveled the garden' and said, 'That's good! I can make sense of my reading by fixing up my mistakes.' Then I would continue to read. Now *you* try the next sentence with a miscue." As Mary rereads the next sentences, the teacher scaffolds her attempts with strategy conversations. He focuses the conversations on the targeted strategies and discusses the active thinking process involved in using a particular strategy or skill. Furthermore, he encourages self-evaluation. For Mary, the teacher says, "I like the way you reread that sentence to correct your mistake. What did you think about as you changed your original response?" This approach engages Mary in describing her thinking. The teacher responds by supporting active thinking and highlighting Mary's strengths in strategy deployment. These on-the-spot conversations help Mary talk about her strategy use as well as expand her strategy options. These conversations lead into another aspect of strategy and skill instruction, self-assessment.

Self-Assessment

Another aspect of strategy and skill instruction is helping students evaluate their increasing use of strategic reading processes. Self-assessment, therefore, directs the students' attention to the use of various strategies and to the effect their implementation has on their reading. It also helps students draw relationships among their strategy use, skill knowledge, and personal effort.

Constructing a graph or self-assessment rubric of strategy use or skill knowledge provides an avenue for the students and teacher to discuss the

Table 3–1   *Chart for Self-Evaluation of Fluency*

How I Read Today	M	T	W	Th	F
Fluently in Phrases					
Mostly in Phrases				•	•
Sometimes Word by Word		•	•		
Mostly Word by Word	•				

Table 3–2   *Chart for Self-Assessment of Comprehension Strategies*

Today when I read,

	Not at All	Sometimes	Most of the Time
I made predictions throughout.			
I revised my predictions as needed.			
I justified my thinking.			
I thought about the information in the text.			
I thought about what I knew.			
I used important information.			
I used the text information and what I knew together.			

Today my reading was _____ because _____

_____.

strategies that the students are using and how the strategies or skills will enhance active reading. For example, using the chart in Table 3–1, Mary evaluated her fluency when she completed her second reading. This evaluation encouraged her to discuss how the strategies she was acquiring were influencing her reading fluency. Thus, Mary, like other students, assumes increasing responsibility for changing her reading behaviors. Charts can be skill-oriented, as in the fluency chart in Table 3–1. Or they can be charts of strategy use, such as the chart in Table 3–2. Self-assessment charts can vary in complexity; however, the focus of charting should be the evaluation of strategy and skill use and discussing how changing strategic reading enhances constructing meaning with text. Thus, students assume the role of monitoring strategic reading; the teacher discusses their troubleshooting strategies, thus encouraging self-assessment.

Teachers must identify those strategies and skills that are limiting active reading. The teacher asks, "What strategies and skills are limiting reading improvement? Will instruction in these strategies or skills advance active reading?" Identifying and working with these strategies and skills will improve overall reading. Therefore, the key characteristic of SAS is the identification of specific strategies and skills that readers need and that, when taught, will enhance constructing meaning with text.

FOCUS OF SKILL AND STRATEGY INSTRUCTION

- Implement strategy and skill instruction.
- Encourage students to employ self-assessment.
- Converse about strategy use.

Personalized Reading and Writing (PRW)

In personalized reading and writing (PRW), students are engaged in 10 to 15 minutes of self-selected reading and writing. This element offers students a time of quiet reflection to respond personally, using the language arts. Writing and reading influence each other and both develop from children's desire to communicate. In this phase, time is set aside for the students and teacher to read and write for their own purposes. Easing the structure of the teaching session and shifting the control to the students are crucial aspects of situating literacy. If the students do not experience "choosing to read and write," they may not define literate activities as a part of their lives. Personal reading and writing allows time for students to define their literacy interest, to read and write for their own purposes, and to read and write without failing because they establish their purposes and their responses. In this way, they are defining themselves as literate individuals.

For the silent reading time students select books, magazines, newspapers, or their own writing to read during the designated time period. Encouraging students to read books for their own enjoyment rather than instructional purposes develops the desire to read. They learn to ask themselves, "What do I want to read about? What kind of stories do I find more interesting?" This facilitates habits of book selection and defining interests (Gambrell & Marinak, 1997).

Students are taught to match the book to their reading levels by using the rule of thumb (Morrow & Walker, 1997). To determine whether it is a good match, they read a page from their selected book and put a finger on each unknown word starting with the little finger. If they reach their thumb before the end of the page, the book is too difficult and another should be selected. Therefore, personalized reading encourages students to select books they can successfully read and moves the control of the selection of reading material from the teacher to the students. In fact, during this element, the students are in control; they have no "have-to" reading. If the students want to skip pages, look at pictures, laugh, or cry, they can read and think whatever they want. The students control what they learn from books.

For personal writing the students and teacher communicate through writing. During each session, students write to the teacher about anything of interest or importance to them. Following the journal entry, the teacher comments with a brief, personal, and honest reaction to what was written.

The teacher responds during each session to what the students have written. The teacher's comments can be an empathetic response or can ask for more information. Such comments (e.g., "That sounds like fun, I would like to know more about . . . " or "Can you describe what it looked like?") allow the teacher to encourage the fluent writing of ideas without evaluations. The focus is communication between students and teacher; therefore, the teacher should not correct any spelling or grammatical errors.

The teacher encourages the writing of ideas as he models correct writing forms in his responses to the student. This stream-of-consciousness communication is based on the students' personal, real-life experiences. The topics, length, and format are self-selected. As students compose text, they think about ways to express ideas. This thinking about how ideas are expressed sensitizes students to the visual aspects of text (how words are spelled and the order of words in sentences); consequently, students become more aware of how words are used.

In fact, personal reading and writing are both major sources of knowledge about word meaning and sentence and text structure. Both are major vehicles for self-reflection because they encourage students to think about what they want to read and learn as well as what they want to communicate in written form. Further, once students have written their thoughts on paper, they can reflect on their thinking, elaborating their personal ideas.

Thus, personal reading and writing develop within students an interest in reading and writing for their own enjoyment. It releases students from the "have-to" assignments made during explicit and guided instruction, thus placing them in control of their interests, ideas, and emotions. By setting aside time for personal reading and writing, teachers are inviting these readers to be members of the literacy club. As readers continue to read and write for their own purposes, they set their own goals and thus control their responses. A student selects her journal writing to include in her portfolio. Figure 3–1 shows her reflection about why she selected the journal. This activity has no wrong answers—in fact, *no* answers—thus students cannot fail. This time gives students an opportunity to pursue their interests, responding personally to literacy.

FOCUS OF PERSONALIZED READING AND WRITING

- Evoke a personal response.
- Choose reading and writing purposes.
- Provide a failure-free situation.

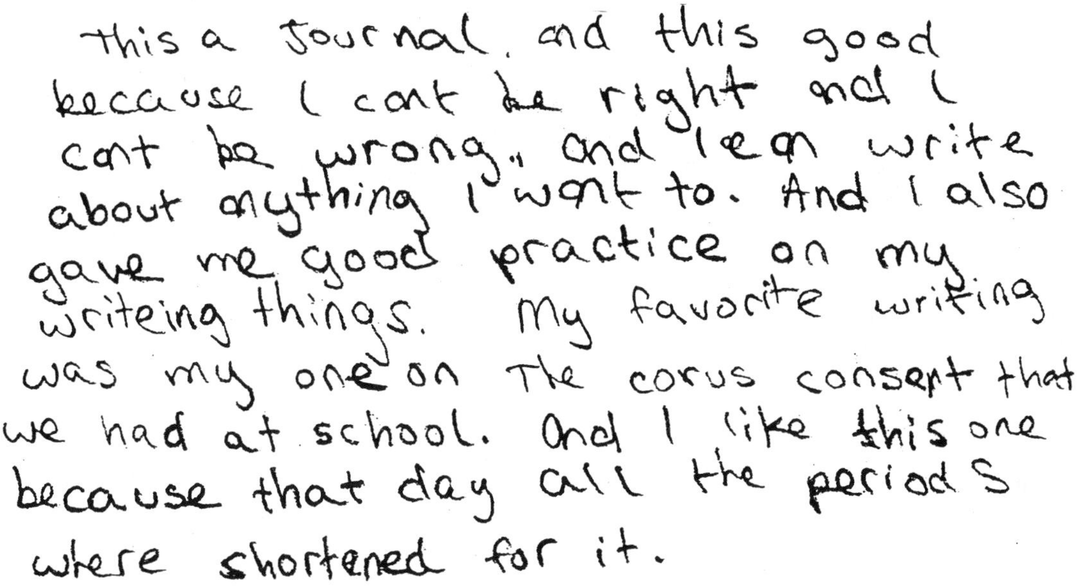

this a Journal, and this good
because I cant be right and I
cant be wrong, and I can write
about anything I want to. And I also
gave me good practice on my
writeing things. My favorite writing
was my one on The corus consert that
we had at school. And I like this one
because that day all the periods
where shortened for it.

Figure 3-1 *Portfolio Reflection About Journal Writing*

Summary

Reflecting on his teaching roles, the teacher plans instruction. *Familiar text time* begins each session with familiar activities that are chosen by the student. It provides time for easy, familiar reading allowing the student to use the strategies and skills she has just learned. During *guided contextual reading*, the teacher guides students' learning; therefore, he is constantly asking what will make this reading event successful for students. As he teaches the planned lesson, he encourages students to read actively by focusing their attention on constructing meaning with text. He probes with leading questions. "What did the author mean when she said that? Does that (the answer) make sense in relation to the other ideas presented in the story?"

During *strategy and skill* instruction, the teacher decides which strategies and skills would, if taught, result in higher reading achievement. Then he develops short demonstration activities to teach strategic reading and converses with students about using strategies. He uses charts to encourage self-assessment and continues the discussion about strategy use. Therefore, he builds responsibility within the students by gradually giving them the control to monitor their own reading behavior. During *personalized reading and writing*, the teacher allows time for students to read and write for their own purposes, thus inviting them to participate in the literate community.

The format of the teaching framework allows the teacher to develop instructional alternatives that fit the strengths and needs of readers. By systematically planning instruction, the teacher provides learning opportunities that enable readers to become independent learners.

4

Gathering Assessment Data

Teachers gather data to formulate hypotheses about the strategies a reader uses to construct meaning. Decisions are made based on data gathered before any instruction and also after instructional adjustments have been made. This chapter focuses on data acquired before the student has received instruction. Such data provide needed information about the independent problem-solving strategies of the learner.

Data are gathered to make initial decisions about instruction through informal reading inventories (a collection of graded passages). These passages are used to determine a level of instruction that is moderately difficult for students. The teacher also establishes the major instructional concern (presenting problem), whether it is print or meaning, by comparing performance when students read orally and silently. These procedures provide detailed information about the reader's strategies for constructing meaning with text. The teacher uses these data to formulate hypotheses about a particular student's instructional needs. This chapter elaborates on these factors: the major presenting problem, an appropriate text level for instruction, and other assessments that can add data to the initial data collection.

Identifying the Major Presenting Problem

The ultimate goal of reading is to construct meaning with text. In this constructive process, both print and meaning processing occur simultaneously. Students combine sources of information and shift between the text, print knowledge, and personal knowledge to figure out what the text says. Meaning processing involves predicting, monitoring, and elaborating the author's intended meaning. Meaning is usually the predominant focus during reading instruction. In other words, when reading, students are constantly striving to construct meaning. On the other hand, print processing involves predicting, monitoring, and elaborating what the words on the page look like. When the

meaning becomes unclear, the reader shifts his attention to a close examination of single words, that is, to print processing. When students read, they
strategically combine all their resources to construct and reconstruct the author's message.

Based on an informal reading inventory, the teacher decides whether
print processing or meaning processing is the major inhibiting factor when
reading becomes difficult. As the teacher works with a student, she asks herself, "What is inhibiting constructing meaning with text? Is the student having
difficulty recognizing the words (print processing), understanding the content
(meaning processing), or both?" She knows reading requires that the student
use both print processing and meaning processing to construct meaning with
text. She also realizes oral reading is a different task from silent reading.

When reading orally, the reader must attend not only to meaning but
also to the oral production of the text. According to Allington (1984, p. 853),
"the instructional setting for oral reading imposes different demands from that
of silent reading (e.g., public vs. private performance, personal vs. external
monitor of performance, emphasis on accuracy of production vs. accuracy of
meaning construction)." If the teacher needs information on print-processing
ability, she uses an oral reading assessment. She observes how the student attends to print when reading breaks down. If reading is impaired by print processing, the teacher listens to the student read orally and asks him questions
to check comprehension, a process known as *oral reading analysis* including
miscue analysis. Some students call words fluently but need assistance in how
to construct meaning with the words that they recognize (meaning processing). If the teacher needs further information on meaning processing, she uses
silent reading analysis and asks the student to think aloud at critical points in
the story. She breaks a story into segments and discusses the story after each
segment. These procedures are known as *silent reading analysis* including
silent reading analysis.

By looking at the pattern in oral reading and silent reading on an informal reading inventory, the teacher can decide which is the major presenting
problem, print or meaning processing. This initial decision merely begins her
analysis of how the student is approaching the reading task. Figure 4–1 illustrates the assessment of the presenting problem. The teacher establishes the
major presenting problem by thinking about how print processing and meaning processing affect the student's reading.

Establishing the Level of Student Performance

To begin gathering data, the teacher samples reading behavior across levels
of text difficulty to identify the student's level of performance. To make this
assessment, the teacher uses a series of graded passages that range in difficulty from first grade to junior high. This procedure is known as *informal
reading assessment.* A reader's responses on easy, moderate, and difficult
texts can be used to determine a level at which the student will experience

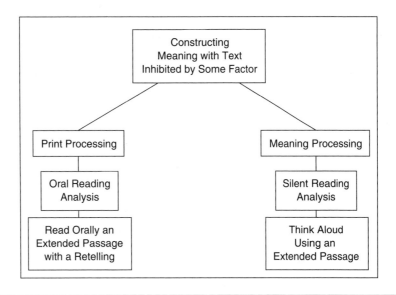

Figure 4–1   *Assessment of Major Presenting Problem*

success in classroom instruction. In the initial assessment, the teacher evaluates both oral and silent reading performance to establish appropriate instructional ranges for oral and silent reading.

Categories of Performance

To determine the level, the diagnostic teacher can administer passages from a standard informal reading inventory (IRI) such as the Basic Reading Inventory (Johns, 2001). Levels of performance can be established for both oral and silent reading, because the inventory has equivalent forms for both types of reading. Therefore, the teacher administers one form for the oral reading analysis and another form for the silent reading analysis. Three estimates of reading performance are derived:

1. The student's independent reading level provides an estimate of the level at which the student can read fluently with a high level of comprehension. The student reads and understands enough of the text to monitor his own reading performance. He applies appropriate correction strategies when reading breaks down, using both reader-based and text-based processing; therefore, teacher-directed instruction is not necessary.

2. The student's instructional reading level provides an estimate of the level at which the student experiences a mild amount of stress between the text and his present reading strategies. It is assumed that

classroom instruction would increase the student's understanding of the text and ability to construct new information with the text.

3. The student's frustration reading level provides an estimate of the level at which the reader is not fluent and has little recall of textual information. It is projected that at this level, guided instruction would be extremely demanding and time-consuming because the reader does not know enough about what he is reading to make adequate connections between the new information and prior knowledge.

These levels are derived by having the student read graded passages as in an informal reading inventory.

Scoring the Informal Reading Inventory

After each passage has been read, comprehension is evaluated by computing the percentage of correct answers to various types of comprehension questions, such as main idea, supporting details, inferences, and vocabulary. As the student reads orally, errors or miscues (deviations from the text) are recorded. These errors are used to compute an error rate, or percentage of word recognition. Although variation exists in what types of errors or miscues are used to compute a score, generally substitutions, mispronunciations, omissions, insertions, and unknown words are used to compute the error rate (see Figure 4–2). Other reading behaviors such as repetitions and self-corrections are analyzed when a qualitative assessment of oral reading performance is conducted and indicate that the reader is constructing meaning. (Further directions for conducting informal reading assessments can be found in the Appendix I.)

Establishing Instructional Level

From the information derived from the informal reading inventory, the teacher identifies a level that would be moderately difficult for the student. She thinks again about the criteria for frustration and independent reading level and mentally pictures the ranges shown in Figure 4–3. Word recognition and comprehension criteria for *independent* reading are 1 miscue in 100 words (1/100 or 99 percent accuracy) and 90 percent comprehension accuracy. When readers know most of the words and concepts, they can then focus their attention on constructing meaning. In other words, they can independently read the text, making a variety of connections between what they know and what's in the text. Other criteria are used to identify text that is extremely difficult for a reader. Word recognition and comprehension criteria for *frustration* reading are 1 miscue in 10 words (1/10 or 90 percent accuracy) and 50 percent comprehension accuracy. Clay (1993) believes that more than a 10 percent error rate represents a "hard" text for a young child. At this frustration level, readers have extreme difficulty constructing meaning for two general reasons.

Substitutions or mispronunciations (the replacement of one word for another): Mark the mispronounced word by drawing a line through it and writing the substitution above the word.

want
"The man ~~went~~ to the store," said Ann.

Omissions (leaving out words): Circle the word omitted.

"The man went to (the) store," said Ann.

Insertions (adding extra words): Draw a carat and write the inserted word above it.

away
"The man went ∧to the store," said Ann.

Transpositions (changing the word order): Mark with a ⌐‾‾‾‾‾.

"The man went to the store," said Ann.

Prompted words (words that have to be prompted or supplied by the teacher): Write the letter *P* above these words.

P
"The man went to the store," said Ann.

Figure 4–2 *Scoreable Errors (to be used in computing error rate)*

Either they don't recognize enough words to correct their miscues and thus regain meaning, or they don't understand enough of the concepts to relate what they are reading to what they know. In either case, readers struggle to regain meaning, but the attempt is futile.

The range of performance between frustration level reading and independent level reading is called the *instructional level,* or more appropriately the *instructional range.* The instructional level is an estimate of the level at which the student would have some problems when reading classroom texts at sight, but most of these problems can be overcome after the student has a chance to read the same text silently. Therefore, the guidelines for regular classroom instruction are more in line with traditional scoring criteria in informal assessment. These criteria use 95 percent accuracy at word identification and 75 percent on comprehension as an estimate of instructional reading level. This instructional range is most appropriate for classroom instruction where less individual support can be provided. The range between independent and frustration level includes both (a) the acceptable instructional level used within a classroom setting and (b) a borderline range, which is often used in one-to-one tutoring. In this borderline range, the reader typically uses active, constructive processes to regain meaning, which often reveal his

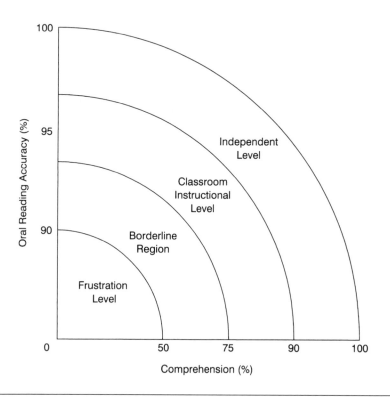

Figure 4–3 *Performance Ranges*

strengths and strategies in meaning construction. As Barr, Blachowicz, and Wogman-Sadow (1995) have pointed out:

> *Students who perform in the borderline region between frustration level and acceptable instructional level may be helped by instruction that has been developed with their particular problem in mind. This borderline region is characterized by an accuracy of 90–94% on oral reading and 50–74% on comprehension questions. (pp. 223–224)*

This borderline region represents a text level that is moderately difficult and is appropriate for one-to-one tutoring. The teacher uses this information to select appropriate materials for instruction (see Chapter 3).

Adding a Fluency Rating

While analyzing the student's performance using the traditional criteria on the informal reading inventory, the teacher can also evaluate the student's fluency as she listens to him read orally. To do so, she asks herself three questions:

1. Is the student's reading fairly smooth?

2. Does the student read words in meaningful phrases?

3. Does the student's pitch, stress, and intonation convey the meaning of the text?

Using these questions, the teacher rates the student's fluency on reading each paragraph and adds this information to that obtained from the traditional informal reading assessment. Sometimes the informal reading inventory does not reveal a problem with oral reading (few substitutions, omissions, or prompts), but the phrasing seems atypical. The student reads "as if print knowledge has not become sufficiently automatic to permit attention to phrasing . . . " (Barr, Blachowicz, & Wogman-Sadow, 1995, p. 58). Thus, print processing must also be evaluated by rating fluency. The teacher notes how the student's oral reading miscues and comprehension interact with his reading fluency on the informal reading assessment. Teachers have used a four-point fluency scale to evaluate upper elementary school children's reading fluency (Zutell, 1988). This scale is a valid and reliable measure of the student's fluent reading and correlates with overall reading ability (Zutell, 1988). The scale includes ratings to reveal patterns of oral reading fluency (see Table 4–1). Using this scale, a student's rating of 1 would indicate that the student is experiencing a great deal of stress and is reading at frustration level. A rating of 2 or 3 would indicate a mild amount of stress and that the student would profit from instruction at this level. A score of 4 would indicate fluent, independent reading. After listening to the students read, the teacher uses the fluency rating in conjunction with the information obtained from the informal reading assessment to identify performance levels and major presenting problems.

Table 4–1   *Ratings for Oral Reading Fluency*

---

1. Clearly labored and disfluent reading, marked by very slow pace (less than 60 wpm), word-by-word reading, numerous pauses, sound-outs, repetitions, and/or lack of intonation and expression.
2. Slow and choppy reading, marked by slow pace (roughly 60–80 wpm), reading in two- and three-word phrases, many pauses, sound-outs, and/or repetitions, some difficulty with phrase, clause, and sentence boundaries and/or intonation problems at the ends of sentences.
3. Poor phrasing and intonation, marked by reasonable pace (roughly 80–105 wpm), but with some choppiness and possibly several repetitions, sound-outs, and/or run-ons.
4. Fairly fluent reading, marked by good pace (more than 110 wpm), longer phrases, and a good sense of expression and intonation. While there may be some difficulties with aspects of fluent reading behavior, this reader is aware of the need for appropriate phrasing and intonation; repetitions may be used to correct phrasing/expression errors.

From: *Developing a Procedure for Assessing Oral Reading Fluency: Establishing Validity and Reliability,* by J. Zutell, May 1988. Paper presented at 33rd Annual Convention, International Reading Association, Toronto, Canada. Reprinted by permission.

Table 4–2   *Criteria for Determining Instructional Reading Levels*

Grade Level of Paragraph	Fluency	Miscue Rate	Oral Comprehension	Silent Comprehension
1–2	2–3	$^1/_{10}$–$^1/_{16}$	65–80%	65–80%
3–5	2–3	$^1/_{13}$–$^1/_{26}$	65–80	65–80
6 +	3–4	$^1/_{18}$–$^1/_{35}$	70–85	70–85

Based on Powell (1981), Clay (1993), and clinical experience.

Analyzing the Results from the Informal Reading Inventory

After administering the informal reading inventory, the teacher analyzes the student's reading performance for both oral and silent reading by summarizing the data on a summary sheet (see Table A–7 in Appendix I). For oral reading, she records the fluency rating, miscue rate, and comprehension percentage for each paragraph given. Likewise, she records comprehension percentages for the silent reading paragraphs given. When she has each paragraph recorded on the summary sheet, she reviews the data to establish an instructional level for both oral and silent reading. This level is indicated by the highest paragraph the student reads at the instructional level before reaching frustration. Using the criteria for performance on the chart in Table 4–2, the teacher establishes independent, instructional, and frustration levels for oral and silent reading as she begins her analysis of oral and silent reading.

When the instructional level for both oral and silent reading has been established, the teacher compares the performance on each set of paragraphs. She thinks about the instructional level for oral reading and silent reading, realizing that she needs to establish a level at which the student will profit from instruction. In the following example, if she uses silent reading, she wonders whether Ricardo will read the words or just skip words and guess at the meaning. She knows that the overall instructional level at which the student will profit from instruction must be established in order to select material. Ricardo's scores were the following:

	Oral Reading	Silent Reading
Independent Level	1.25	2
Instructional Level	1.75	3
Frustration Level	2	4

Reviewing Ricardo's performance, the teacher established the instructional level at the end of first grade because oral reading was lower than silent reading. Thus, Ricardo's major presenting problem is print processing. At the end of first grade, Ricardo will read at least 90 percent of the words correctly and use meaning and print clues to revise his miscues. To be sure that Ricardo is using both print and meaning processing to construct meaning with text, the teacher looks for instructional material at the end of first grade to use during guided contextual reading. At this instructional level, Ricardo will be able to use both print processing and meaning processing. She selected *Marvin Redpost: Lost at Birth*, with a reading level estimated near the end of first grade. She hypothesized that at this level, Ricardo would be able to use both print and meaning processes as he reads. From the data, she can also conclude that Ricardo is more proficient at silent reading than oral reading. Using the chart at the beginning of the chapter, the teacher hypothesizes that the student's strength is in meaning processing and that he needs support for print processing. She begins to build a program of instruction using his strength in meaning processing during guided contextual reading (see Chapter 3) and works on print processing during strategy and skill instruction.

As the teacher gathers data about performance levels, she is also thinking about the strategies the student is using. The teacher can conduct further assessments to analyze the reader's strategies and skills.

Further Assessments

After the teacher has completed the informal reading inventory, she continues gathering diagnostic data and begins to interpret her initial findings. The first interpretation is likely to be the stage of reading development indicated by the informal reading inventory. Using the instructional reading level ascertained by the informal reading inventory, the teacher determines the stage of reading development for the child. To do this, she reviews the informal reading inventory for patterns of strengths and decides on the highest level paragraph that met the instructional criteria. She then compares this level to the stages of reading development. As she compares the information from the informal reading inventory matching it with the stages of reading development, she asks herself if further assessments would add information for adjusting instruction to meet the reader's needs. If the further assessments are too time-consuming, she continues with an instructional plan observing the characteristics of the reader at the stage. In other words, she can gather information while observing children within the instructional environment. However, other times she may want further assessments to elaborate her decisions about instruction. In this case, the teacher reviews the informal reading inventory and the stages of reading development to find a level and stage of reading for a child. From this information, the teacher selects further assessments that will inform her about the child's abilities.

Stages of Reading Development

Teachers can use stages to represent ways to group the progression of understandings that occur during reading development. Four stages help the teacher understand the major tasks confronting her students as they develop as readers (Walker, 2003). The stages are not static but rather are overlapping stages of development that flow along a continuum. During the transition from one stage to the next, critical learning occurs. At this time, readers refine and build on their experience with previous tasks, fitting the resulting insights into the new framework as it develops. During this overlap or interface, students begin to take control of their learning while at the same time they encounter text that requires new strategies. They are assimilating new strategies while taking control over familiar strategies. Figure 4–4 elaborates the stages.

The first stage of reading, often called the *emergent literacy stage*, begins at a very young age and continues to the middle of first grade. Children at this stage encounter literacy in social situations with their families and teachers. As they interact with others, they begin to understand what literacy is. Children read along with parents and friends and begin to understand what a book is. After memorizing a few books, often students can recognize a few words. This is the beginning of a recognition or sight vocabulary. Thus, their literacy emerges out of the social situations in which they encounter literacy.

As developing readers begin to encounter more unfamiliar words and longer stories, they develop new strategies to meet the challenges of the second stage which begins during first grade and continues through second grade. To figure out unfamiliar words, they use decoding analogies where they match consistent letter-sound patterns in words they know with unfamiliar words. Likewise, their literacy development becomes grounded in textual conventions like patterns in stories, and their comprehension relies less on understanding the social context and more on the story organization.

As learners encounter longer passages and chapter books where word meanings are embedded in complex sentence structures, the simple strategies of using sight words, decoding by analogy, and retelling the facts of a story

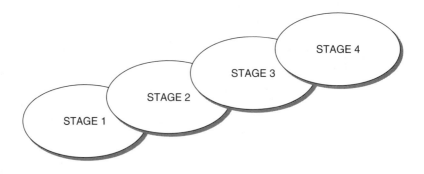

Figure 4–4 *Stages of Reading Development*

are no longer sufficient. They are entering the third stage that begins during third grade and continues through fifth grade. At this stage, the sentences have expanded, becoming longer and more complex. During this stage, the students focus on the forms of the sentences and match them with what they know about word and story meaning. As students continue to progress and read more challenging text, they find the strategies that deal primarily with textual information are no longer adequate.

In the fourth stage that begins in sixth grade and continues through eighth grade, texts are more difficult because authors develop complex ideas. Thus, readers assert new control over their thinking as they begin experimenting with ways of thinking. Readers must begin to shift strategically between text-based and reader-based processing, synthesizing their understanding of text.

In the next section, each stage will be discussed and a few selected assessments will be suggested that augment the teacher's understanding of the readers' approach to literacy.

Stage One

Many younger children may not have scored within the independent or instructional range on any paragraph on the informal reading inventory. Thus, they fall within stage one. They need further assessments to ascertain what they know. During this stage, young readers' knowledge about printed texts expands as parents read books to them. Children begin to read along with their parents, memorizing the book. As they do this, they begin to understand that they are reading from the left side of the page to the right side of the page. They also begin to notice that books are read from the top of the page to the bottom. These new associations are what we term *concepts of print* and are important features of emergent literacy. As young children watch TV and go out to eat with their families, they begin to read signs based on distinctive features like the *M* in McDonalds. They know that when they go to the golden arches, they are going to eat hamburgers and French fries. This is an indication they are noticing that print carries meaning. Their knowledge grows as young children move the awareness that the golden *M* in McDonalds stands for *M* to understand that *m* is in many words and we call it a letter. This understanding of letter names demonstrates that children know letters are a major component of print. Young children also memorize nursery rhymes and in this way begin to hear sounds in words. Initially, they notice the rhyming sounds in words and how many sounds are in a word. In this stage, they also begin to understand concepts about words—that printed words have meaning, begin with certain letters, and have letter-sound patterns that always stay the same. This concept of word is another essential part of the concepts about print assessment.

Concepts About Print

As children read books with others, they begin to notice some basic conventions about written language. We call these early understandings *concepts about print.* They involve such things as understanding what we read (the printed words), where the print begins, what a printed word is, and reading left to right. They also involve the notion that print carries meaning. In assessing concepts about print teachers can use any simple picture book. While looking at the book, the teacher asks the child a series of questions about book knowledge (see Table 4–3).

Speech to Print Match

There are two ways of evaluating voice to print match. The first is more in line with concepts about print, and the other way is leading into knowledge of letter names. One way is simply to read a line of print and have the student follow along, pointing to each word as you read it. This indicates an understanding that words are the unit that we read. The young child understands that the marks on the page are related to what you are reading. Another similar emerging ability that precedes actual reading is being able to repeat a line of print with the appropriate number of words. Reading all the words correctly is not important; the child simply repeats the sentence, retaining the meaning and sentence length. This knowledge is prerequisite to understanding that individual words and letters make up words.

Knowledge of Letter Names

Another assessment for young children is knowledge of letter names. As they notice the distinctive features within their social environment, young children

Table 4–3   *Concepts About Print Interview*

---

1. Holding the picture book by its spine, ask the child to show you the front of the book, or where it begins.
2. Say that you are going to read the story. Ask the child where to begin the story. This indicates that you are going to read the print, not the pictures in the story.
3. On the next page, ask the child to point where you should begin and in what direction should you go. This indicates the child's understanding about directionality or that print is read from the left side of the page to the right side.
4. After you have read that line, ask the child to indicate where to go next. The child should indicate that you should make a return sweep and begin on the next line. This indicates that print is read from top to bottom.
5. You can also ask where to stop reading on this page, which also indicates going from top to bottom.
6. Next, turn the page to a double spread of print. Ask the child which page you read first.
7. A child who is more advanced should be able to indicate information about words. Ask the child to frame one word, then two words.
8. Ask the child to point to the beginning letter in a word, any letter in a word.
9. Finally, ask the child to name any letters they know and any words they know.

---

also notice the distinctive features of words, which are the letters. At the outset, they learn the letters in their own name so they can write it. As parents and teachers talk about letters in words and the alphabet, young children begin to associate the various letters with their names. They often know that "-S-T-O-P" spells stop and spell it every time they see a red hexagon sign with the same letters. They learn from various encounters where their parents or teachers repeatedly point out the letters and say the letter names. As they learn the letters, they are able to read a few words. The teacher assesses letter names to indicate how the child is noticing the features of words (see Table 4–4).

Knowledge of letter names assessed before first grade has consistently been the best predictor of success in reading at the end of first grade. Many informal reading inventories include an informal assessment for letter names where the child simply says the name of the letter as the teacher points to the letter and records the student's response. This assessment indicates how the child is using the distinctive features of words to differentiate knowledge about letters that are found in words. If the student is not attending to the distinctive features of letters within words, particularly the initial letter, then all words look alike, and the student has difficulty figuring out individual words.

Phonological Awareness

Another area the teacher can assess is the young child's phonological awareness. This awareness develops on three levels; the syllable, the rime-onset level, and the phoneme level (Goswami, 2000). As children hear familiar stories read repeatedly, they begin to associate certain words with certain sound chunks. This ability leads to hearing the syllables in words like "You can't catch me. I'm the Gingerbread Man." Children recognize that Gingerbread has more than one syllable. This is the first level of phonological awareness. Children also begin to hear the rhymes in words. As children listen to nursery rhymes and jingles, they begin to associate the singsong, quality heard with the rhymes they hear. As they repeatedly chime in with the nursery rhyme "Jack and Jill went up the hill," they begin to notice that *Jill* and *hill* share some of the same sounds, /ill/. The more stories and rhymes they memorize, the more they begin to recognize the sound structure of language until they notice that Jack and Jill both begin with the same sound. Recognizing the initial sound leads the way to noticing the initial phoneme and rimes in a word. This is called the *onset* (the initial phoneme) and *rime* (the letters following

Table 4–4   *Knowledge of Letter Names*

The teacher points to a letter and asks the child to say its name.

t	n	d	f	a	s	k	b	m	g
c	r	l	h	p	x	v	o	z	y

the initial phoneme) in words. Onset and rime awareness is another aspect of acquiring the alphabetic principle. This second level of understanding phonological awareness adds to the young child's ability to develop a fund of readily recognized words. Later in the next stage of reading development, the third level of phonological awareness will develop. The child will recognize more individual phonemes in words as he begins to read more words in stories. However, this is far more abstract than noticing rhymes. As the individual sounds in words often merge together, understanding individual sounds in words often merge together, understanding individual sounds is difficult at this stage and develops during the next stage.

The teacher assesses phonological awareness to ascertain what levels of sound knowledge the young child has. Phonological awareness indicates that the young child has developed understandings about how sounds work in words. Many informal reading inventories include an informal assessment for phonological awareness. The teacher simply says a word and asks what the beginning sound is or how many sounds they hear in the word (see Table 4–5).

To continue the assessment, the teacher says two words and asks if they rhyme. The teacher records the student's responses. This assessment indicates how the child is using his knowledge of sounds in words to understand one of the concepts about words: Words have sound patterns that stay the same every time the word is said or read (see Table 4–6).

Putting Stage One Assessments to Work

Using these assessments along with the informal reading inventory, the teacher plans literacy activities. Since a child at this stage usually does not have a score from the informal reading inventory, the teacher selects easy, predictable books for shared reading or uses language experience (see Part Two for shared reading and language experience techniques) for the guided

Table 4–5   *Assessment of Phonological Awareness–Syllable Level*

Say the word and ask the child how many syllables he hears.

| pat | patting | hot | puddle | batter | mat | walking | giraffe |

Table 4–6   *Assessment of Phonological Awareness–Rime-Onset Level*

Do the two words rhyme? Do they have the same sounds at the end of the word?

pat, hat	hot, not	bat, sit	cake, snake
went, sent	pit, bark	toad, road	cat, cake
sheep, soak	meet, sweet	rain, pain	boy, toy

contextual reading (see Chapter 3). Using the information from the assessment, she may decide either to do some letter naming activities or sound building activities or both during the strategy or skill lesson (see Chapter 3). In addition to these activities, she selects easy, predictable books that can be learned quickly and read repeatedly to develop a fund of words recognized by sight.

Stage Two

Because the students can read longer stories, they encounter unfamiliar words that are not contained in their sight vocabularies. Therefore, emerging readers develop new ways to figure out unfamiliar words. As children participate in literacy activities, their recognition vocabulary increases. Along with this increasing word identification, children begin to read longer stories; therefore, reading changes from a shared oral experience to silent reading and discussion. Initially, the children are familiar with most words in stories because many of the stories are encountered during shared oral reading before reading alone. These known words represent their sight word vocabulary. This ability to identify words allows the children to figure out unfamiliar words using the oral context created by the shared experience. If they use distinctive features of words, they usually look at only the initial letter and then think about what the story means or glance at the picture to figure out the word.

With longer stories, children can no longer rely on pictures as there are fewer of them and many of them do not represent the words on the page. Neither can young children rely on shared understandings to figure out the words as the stories are much too complex for the shared understanding to signify specific words. Therefore, children begin to look for letter patterns in unfamiliar words and map those letter patterns to familiar sound patterns in already known words. This is known as *decoding by analogy.*

As more and more stories are read silently, young children want to communicate their understanding by discussing with others. This discussion initially focuses on retelling what hapenned in the story; therefore, children's knowledge of story grammar is important to assess.

Word Identification

As young children read along with adults, they begin to recognize a few words. These words become more familiar as they repeatedly appear in the text that is read together. Finally, these words become part of the child's sight word vocabulary. Recognizing these words is known as *word identification.* Word identification ability is often used to estimate a reading level. Most informal reading inventories include a word identification assessment, which includes lists of words representing frequent words at a particular grade level. To administer the assessment, you simply ask the child to pronounce each word on the word list. These lists are read until the student misses around 7–10 words in a row. This usually indicates that few words at the more advanced levels will be recognized. The score is the number of words pronounced correctly. The highest level before the student stopped is usually considered the grade level where instruction would be most appropriate. This level is where you can begin your informal reading assessment or this can be used to monitor progress in word identification. This ability to identify words provides an understanding of how the student can recognize words in a passage or story and an indication of the fund of words that can be used to develop phonemic awareness.

Phonemic Awareness

As children begin to look for letter patterns in unfamiliar words and map those letter patterns to familiar letter-sound patterns in already known words, they engage in decoding by analogy. Thus, young children begin to develop phonic knowledge by recognizing rime patterns in words. This builds on their oral phonological abilities that developed in stage one. As children begin to recognize more words at sight, their spontaneous use of decoding analogies grows. Knowledge of the printed words helps to develop a fund of decoding analogies based on onset and rime patterns that are needed to decode unfamiliar words automatically.

Children are also increasing in the third level of phonological awareness—that is, the recognition of more individual phonemes in words. This is far more abstract than noticing rhymes. As the individual sounds in words often merge together, understanding individual sounds is difficult. However, the increase in rime analogies and word recognition facilitates the awareness of phonemes. Phoneme awareness and phonic knowledge in this stage depend highly on phoneme strategies. Segmenting words into their single letter sounds and synthesizing the sounds to form words are strategies used when decoding unfamiliar words. These abilities lead the way to decoding words by using single letter sounds. Children use this ability in combination with decoding analogies to figure out longer, more complex words. The ability to segment sounds and synthesize sounds can be easily measured. Hallie Yopp and Harry Singer (Yopp, 1995) prepared an easy-to-administer test for phoneme segmentation, which includes 22 words and asks students to say the individual phoneme (see Table 4–7). The teacher says the word *sat,* and students say the sounds /s/ /a/ /t/. Each word where the phonemes are correctly identified receives a point. Students who correctly respond to 10 items are still developing their understanding of individual phonemes, while those who score 20 are capable of using individual phonemes to decode unfamiliar words.

Spelling Assessments

One of the best ways to evaluate phonic knowledge is to analyze children's spelling. As they spell words, children must think about each letter and its sound and then synthesize these sounds into words. Thus, spelling is closely linked to phonic knowledge. Children's early spelling that differs in systematic ways from standard spelling can provide some indications of their thinking about how sounds work in words. Thus, the level of spelling development

Table 4–7   *Yopp-Singer Test of Phoneme Segmentation*

Name _____   Date _____

Score (number correct) _____

Directions: Today we're going to play a word game. I'm going to say a word and I want you to break the word apart. You are going to tell me each sound in the word in order. For example, if I say "old," you should say "/o/-/l/-/d/." (Administrator: Be sure to say the sounds, not the letters, in the word.) Let's try a few together.

Practice items: (Assist the child in segmenting these items as necessary.) ride, go, man

Test items: (Circle those items that the student correctly segments; incorrect responses may be recorded on the blank line following the item.)

1.	dog	_____	12.	lay	_____
2.	keep	_____	13.	race	_____
3.	fine	_____	14.	zoo	_____
4.	no	_____	15.	three	_____
5.	she	_____	16.	job	_____
6.	wave	_____	17.	in	_____
7.	grew	_____	18.	ice	_____
8.	that	_____	19.	at	_____
9.	red	_____	20.	top	_____
10.	me	_____	21.	by	_____
11.	sat	_____	22.	do	_____

gives insight into their knowledge and use of phonics. The teacher uses the levels of spelling development to ascertain the child's spelling patterns and use of phonic knowledge. Gillet and Temple (1994) suggest four levels of spelling development. The first level of spelling development is the prephonemic level where no letter-sound relationships are present. Children denote words by letters but the spellings have no similarity to correct spellings. They often write a single letter or number to indicate a word. This does show that they understand the print carries meaning. Children at the second level, the early phonemic level, represent some of the sounds in words in a systematic way. They might represent the word *net* with the letters *nt.* Vowels are seldom present in their writing. At the third level, the letter-naming level, letter sounds represent more than half the sounds. The actual word produced when saying the letters actually sounds like the word as in spelling *net* as *nat.* The transitional stage is where spelling is fairly standard, with a vowel in every syllable; however, the spelling does not conform to the correct spelling. Finally, the teacher recognizes that some words can be spelled correctly. To assess spelling, the teacher has the students write a paragraph or two and collects this writing sample. Then, the teacher can rate each word according to the rubric based on the levels of spelling development (see Table 4–8).

In this rubric, the prephonemic level equals 0, early phonemic level equals 1, letter-naming level equals 2, the transitional level equals 3, and the correct spelling equals 4. After rating each word, the teacher can add the ratings together and divide by the number of words in the written passage. The average score gives an approximate level for spelling and phonic knowledge. Children in this stage can show any type of pattern. However, most children in this stage will have the majority of the spellings at the letter-name level.

Another way to assess spelling is to give a list of spelling words and compare the individual spellings of the words to levels of spelling development and figure out a spelling level. Bear, Invernizzi, Templeton, and Johnston (2000) have developed a test that uses 22 words to evaluate spelling through the grades. For the purposes of identifying phonic knowledge during this stage, only the first 10 words need to be used. They are *bed, ship, drive, bump, when, train, closet, chase, float,* and *beaches.* How students spell these words can be compared to the stages of spelling development mentioned previously. The teacher also can use the detailed analysis provided in the book *Words Their Way* (Bear et al., 2000) to interpret the spelling test and decide on instructional procedures.

Table 4–8   *Spelling Assessment Rubric*

---

0 = Prephonemic Stage
Random letters depict a message and show some knowledge of top-bottom and left-to-right concept
No letter-sound relationship present
Uses and repeats known letters and numbers (prefers uppercase letters)
1 = Early Phonemic Stage
Words are depicted by one or more letters showing a left-to-right order
The letters represent some of the sounds in words, but not all
This letter-naming strategy is erratic and restricted
2 = Letter-Naming Stage
Entire words are present with a majority of the letters
The word has more than half the sounds in the word
Letters are based on sounds as student hears them (invented spelling)
3 = Transitional Stage
Conventional spellings are used properly but not accurately (e.g., *candel* for *candle*)
Spelling is based on standard spelling rather than invented spelling
Vowels appear in every syllable
4 = Correct Spelling

Story Retelling

Another assessment for this stage of literacy is to find out how children understand a story. As children move from oral shared reading, they begin to read silently and, therefore, communicate their story understanding by retelling the story. This is a developing ability, and the teacher wants to ascertain whether the student is continuing his literacy development by also understanding the meaning of the story. The teacher has the student orally retell the story or has the student write a story summary. This retelling can be evaluated by observing and rating the story retelling using a retelling rubric (Table 4–9).

Table 4–9   *Retelling Assessment*

Setting

4	Has an elaborated explanation of setting, including introduction, names of major characters, important places and times
3	Has major character and other characters; briefly describes place and time
2	Has major character and mentions times or places
1	Contains only one idea, such as place, or names minor characters
0	Does not contain any ideas related to setting

Problem

4	Describes the major character's main goal or problem to be solved, including theme of the story; also describes the event that sets up the problem in the story
3	Describes main problem the major character needs to solve
2	Mentions briefly the problem
1	Has an insignificant problem
0	Does not describe any problem

Events

4	Elaborates key story events. Most events are related to working out the problem, are a consequence of this event, or are a character's reaction
3	Has key story events, some of which are related to working out the problem, a consequence of this event, or a character's reaction
2	Describes briefly some key story events
1	Has only a few insignificant events
0	Has no events

Resolution

4	Ends with a feeling of continuity and tells how the problem was solved
3	Ends with a feeling of continuity and briefly tells how the problem was solved
2	Ends with a feeling of continuity, but does not tell how the problem was solved
1	Ends abruptly
0	Ends in the middle of the story

From: *Interactive Handbook for Understanding Reading Diagnosis: A Problem-Solving Approach Using Case Studies* (p. 123) by K. Roskos and B. J. Walker, 1994, Upper Saddle River, N.J.: Merrill/Prentice Hall. Copyright 1994 by Prentice Hall. Adapted by permission.

Using the rubric, the teacher evaluates what information the students tell about the setting, including the place and the characters. The teacher also evaluates how elaborate the students' retelling of the problem is and how extensive is the understanding of key story events. Finally, the teacher evaluates how students end the retelling. In addition to listening to an oral retelling, the teacher can have the class write a story summary and use the same rubric to evaluate the written story summary.

Putting Stage Two Assessments to Work

Using these assessments along with the informal reading inventory, the teacher plans literacy activities. Since the student is at the second stage of reading development, the teacher reviews the informal reading inventory to decide the level of text to be used during guided contextual reading (see Chapter 3). She selects a story, chapter book, or basal reader whose range is near the end of first grade or second grade, depending on the results of the informal reading inventory. If the student is at the second-grade level, the teacher has the student read silently. Using the information from the assessments, she may decide what to do during the strategy or skill lesson. If the major presenting problem is print processing, then she would look under the word attack column in Chapter 5. She might select "Making Words" (see Part Two) to work on phonic knowledge and phoneme awareness. If the major presenting problem is comprehension, then she would look under literal comprehension. She might select the story map technique (see Part Two).

Stage Three

In stage three, children associate their knowledge about print and a particular topic with what is written in sentences. As they progressed through the first two stages, they developed extensive knowledge about the use of decoding analogies and patterns in stories. Now their focus shifts from developing this knowledge to using it as they read. During this stage, readers use sentence sense to increase both their fluency and sentence comprehension. In particular, students learn that words can be grouped together to make thought units and sentences have predictable structures that influence meaning. Sentence comprehension also enhances print processing; therefore, students use sentence context as well as decoding by analogy to figure out unknown words. Using sentence context to figure out unknown words and simultaneously associating appropriate word meanings becomes a major challenge during this stage.

Fluency Assessment

After analyzing the results from the informal reading inventory, the teacher might want to analyze the student's fluency. The teacher prepares a passage that is at the student's instructional reading level and asks the student to read it orally. The teacher can use the same four-point fluency scale (Zutell, 1988) used while gathering information using an informal reading inventory. The scale includes ratings to reveal patterns of oral reading fluency (see Table 4–2). Using this scale, a student's rating of 1 would indicate that the student is experiencing a great deal of stress and is reading at frustration level. A rating of 2 or 3 would indicate a mild amount of stress and that the student would profit from instruction at this level. A score of 4 would indicate fluent, independent reading.

The multidimensional fluency scale (Zutell & Rasinski, 1991) might be preferred to the four-point scale as it measures dimensions of fluency that could lead to the development of an instructional program. In this scale, the teacher assesses the following aspects of fluency: phrasing, smoothness, and pace. Each of these areas is measured on a four-point scale. The teacher has the child read orally and records the reading so she can use the tape to score the dimensions of fluency. Table 4–10 shows how to rate the three dimensions.

Table 4–10   *Multidimensional Fluency Scale*

Phrasing
1. Monotonic with little sense of phrase boundaries, frequent word-by-word reading.
2. Frequent two- and three-word phrases giving the impression of choppy reading; improper stress and intonation that fails to mark ends of sentences and clauses.
3. Mixture of run-ons, mid-sentence pauses for breath, and possibly some choppiness; reasonable stress/intonation.
4. Generally well phrased, mostly in clause and sentence units, with adequate attention to expression.

Smoothness
1. Frequent extended pauses, hesitations, false starts, sound-outs, repetitions, and/or multiple attempts.
2. Several "rough spots" in text where extended pauses, hesitations, etc., are more frequent and disruptive.
3. Occasional breaks in smoothness caused by difficulties with specific words and/or structures.
4. Generally smooth with some breaks, but word and structure difficulties are resolved quickly, usually through self-correction.

Pace
1. Slow and laborious
2. Moderately slow
3. Uneven mixture of fast and slow reading
4. Consistently conversational

From: "Training Teachers to Attend to Their Students' Oral Reading Fluency," by J. Zutell and T. Rasinski, 1991, *Theory into Practice*, 30(3), 211–217. Reprinted by permission. Copyright 1991 by the College of Education, The Ohio State University. All rights reserved.

Using either of these scales, the teacher can readily select techniques for instruction. If phrasing is low, the teacher selects techniques like chunking (see Part Two) to focus on thought units to group words so that meaning is held intact. If smoothness is low, the teacher selects techniques like choral reading (see Part Two) where the smoothness carries the message of the text. If pace is low, the teacher selects techniques like repeated readings (see Part Two) to improve the rate of readings.

Cloze Test

Using sentence context to figure out unknown words and simultaneously associating appropriate meanings is important at this stage. Children at this stage need to learn how the sentence structure influences meaning. To evaluate sentence comprehension, a cloze test can be used. A cloze test consists of a passage with blanks so that the reader uses the sentence context to supply the most credible response. To construct a cloze test, the teacher selects a passage that is 300 words long and is at the beginning of a chapter so that previous text knowledge will not be needed. The teacher then deletes every fifth word after the first sentence. The first and last sentences are left intact. The teacher makes sure the blanks are a consistent length. Readers are provided sufficient time to complete the task so that they work at their own pace. To score the cloze test, the teacher counts only the verbatim responses as correct. Misspelled words are acceptable. Finally, the teacher calculates the percentage of exact responses by dividing the number of correct responses by the number of deletions, which should be 50. This percentage is compared with the criteria for performance: independent 60%–100%, instructional 40%–59%, frustration 0%–39%.

Putting Stage Three Assessments to Work

Using these assessments along with the informal reading inventory, the teacher plans literacy activities. The teacher reviews the informal reading inventory to decide the level of text to be used during guided contextual reading (see Chapter 3). She selects a story, chapter book, or basal reader that is at the instructional level from the informal reading inventory. From the specific assessments, she may decide what to do during the strategy or skill lesson (see Chapter 3). If the major presenting problem is print processing, then she would look under the fluency column in Chapter 5. She might select the repeated reading technique (see Part Two) to work on print and meaning processing simultaneously. If the major presenting problem is comprehension, then she would look under literal comprehension and word meaning columns in Chapter 5. She might select the contextual processing (see Part Two) to improve sentence comprehension.

Stage Four

As students read more difficult text, they find that strategies dealing primarily with information that is in the text are no longer adequate. As they reach this level of text difficulty, they need to use a deeper processing of text. In texts at this level of difficulty, readers construct complex ideas that require an interpretation of text-based information within a reader's personal worldview (Alexander & Jetton, 2000). These processes require the flexible control of strategies. During this stage, children assert new control over their thinking. According to Pressley (2000), sustained strategy instruction produces better test scores for comprehension and more thoughtful readers. The strategy instruction programs focus on multiple strategies for understanding and interpreting texts. Although readers have been using some basic strategies, this stage marks the onset of taking control over multiple strategy use. Some of these strategies include using the title to predict what's going to happen, revising predictions, making new predictions, imagining pictures of information, picking out important points, summarizing important ideas, and rereading to clarify confusing parts. One of the more powerful strategies is the readers' ability to take control of the shift and integration of prior knowledge and the text.

The informal reading inventory provided information about literal and nonliteral comprehension. However, at this stage of literacy development, a key focus is assessing readers' strategies. Therefore, it is important to evaluate the strategies that students do possess. However, the underlying strategies used to construct meaning are internal processes. Since these are internal actions, they are more difficult to assess.

Think-Aloud Assessment

One way to assess the reader's strategic control of meaning construction is to evaluate the shift between prior knowledge and the text. To do this, the teacher can have students think aloud as they read. In this procedure, the teacher divides a story into sections. After the student reads a section silently, he thinks aloud about the story. The teacher prompts by asking him questions and making statements such as: "Tell me what happened. What do you think will happen next? Why do you think that?" The teacher records the student's responses to these questions after each section and then reviews the think-aloud to evaluate whether the student used the text or background knowledge when he summarized, predicted, and elaborated understanding.

Self-Report of Strategy Use

Another way to assess strategy awareness and use is by using a self-report. In a self-report, students are asked which strategies they use and how often they use these strategies to understand and remember information. Teachers can make a checklist with the names of strategies to have students report about their strategy use (see example in Table 4–11).

Similar to a teacher-made checklist where students use self-report to reveal their strategy use is the *Metacognitive Awareness of Reading Strategies Inventory* (Mokhtari & Reichard, 2002), which is based on responses from a large sample size. While taking the instrument the students become aware of

Table 4–11   *Strategy Self-Report*

When I read, I

_____ thought about my purpose for reading.
_____ made predictions.
_____ checked the text.
_____ summarized important points.
_____ compared what I knew with the text.
_____ revised my thinking as I needed.
_____ elaborated what was in the text with what I knew.

the strategies they use as they read. The teacher uses the information to get a general sense of the students' awareness and use of reading strategies as well as over- or underreliance on particular strategies. For example, a student who reports overusing the dictionary may have a limited view of reading, while a student who reports rereading may not know how to use other strategies like summarization. The scale provides a rating for global strategies like setting a purpose, problem-solving strategies like reading slowly and carefully, and support strategies like paraphrasing (see Tables 4–12 and 4–13).

Along with the self-report teachers can interview students and observe their strategy use. The following questions can guide the interview:

1. What do you do before reading to help you understand?

2. While you read, what do you do if you don't understand something?

3. After you read, what do you do to help you remember ideas?

These questions along with self-report checklists and observations during think-aloud can help the teacher identify strategy use.

Putting Stage Four Assessments to Work

Using these assessments along with the informal reading inventory, the teacher plans activities for the teaching framework. Reviewing the informal reading inventory, the teacher identifies an instructional range and selects texts within that range for guided contextual reading (see Chapter 3). Using the information from the think-aloud and self-report assessments, the teacher selects specific strategies to work on during strategy and skill instruction (see Chapter 3). For instance, using information from a think-aloud, she might focus on justifying predictions using textual information. Using information from the self-report, she might decide to instruct students in how to use summarization (see Part Two) to identify important information to remember.

Table 4–12   *Metacognitive Awareness of Reading Strategies Inventory (MARSI, Version 1.0)*

Directions: Listed below are statements about what people do when they read *academic* or *school-related materials* such as textbooks or library books. Five numbers follow each statement (1, 2, 3, 4, 5), and each number means the following:

- **1** means "I **never or almost never** do this."
- **2** means "I do this **only occasionally.**"
- **3** means "I **sometimes** do this" (about 50% of the time).
- **4** means "I **usually** do this."
- **5** means "I **always or almost always** do this."

After reading each statement, **circle the number** (1, 2, 3, 4, 5) that applies to you using the scale provided. Please note that there are **no right or wrong answers** to the statements in this inventory.

Strategy	Scale				
1. I have a purpose in mind when I read.	1	2	3	4	5
2. I take notes while reading to help me understand what I read.	1	2	3	4	5
3. I think about what I know to help me understand what I read.	1	2	3	4	5
4. I preview the text to see what it's about before reading it.	1	2	3	4	5
5. When text becomes difficult, I read aloud to help me understand what I read.	1	2	3	4	5
6. I summarize what I read to reflect on important information in the text.	1	2	3	4	5
7. I think about whether the content of the text fits my reading purpose.	1	2	3	4	5
8. I read slowly but carefully to be sure I understand what I'm reading.	1	2	3	4	5
9. I discuss what I read with others to check my understanding.	1	2	3	4	5
10. I skim the text first by noting characteristics like length and organization.	1	2	3	4	5
11. I try to get back on track when I lose concentration.	1	2	3	4	5
12. I underline or circle information in the text to help me remember it.	1	2	3	4	5
13. I adjust my reading speed according to what I'm reading.	1	2	3	4	5
14. I decide what to read closely and what to ignore.	1	2	3	4	5
15. I use reference materials such as dictionaries to help me understand what I read.	1	2	3	4	5
16. When text becomes difficult, I pay closer attention to what I'm reading.	1	2	3	4	5
17. I use tables, figures, and pictures in text to increase my understanding.	1	2	3	4	5
18. I stop from time to time and think about what I'm reading.	1	2	3	4	5
19. I use context clues to help me better understand what I'm reading.	1	2	3	4	5
20. I paraphrase (restate ideas in my own words) to better understand what I read.	1	2	3	4	5
21. I try to picture or visualize information to help remember what I read.	1	2	3	4	5
22. I use typographical aids like boldface and italics to identify key information.	1	2	3	4	5
23. I critically analyze and evaluate the information presented in the text.	1	2	3	4	5
24. I go back and forth in the text to find relationships among ideas in it.	1	2	3	4	5
25. I check my understanding when I come across conflicting information.	1	2	3	4	5
26. I try to guess what the material is about when I read.	1	2	3	4	5
27. When text becomes difficult, I reread to increase my understanding.	1	2	3	4	5
28. I ask myself questions I like to have answered in the text.	1	2	3	4	5
29. I check to see if my guesses about the text are right or wrong.	1	2	3	4	5
30. I try to guess the meaning of unknown words or phrases.	1	2	3	4	5

From: "Assessing Students' Metacognitive Awareness of Reading Strategies" by K. Mokhtari and C. Reichard, 2002, *Journal of Educational Psychology, 94*(2), 249–259. Copyright 2002 by the American Psychological Association. All rights reserved.

Table 4–13 *Scoring Rubric for MARSI*

Student name: _____ Age: _____ Date: _____
Grade in school: ❏ 6ᵗʰ   ❏ 7ᵗʰ   ❏ 8ᵗʰ   ❏ 9ᵗʰ   ❏ 10ᵗʰ   ❏ 11ᵗʰ   ❏ 12ᵗʰ   ❏ Other

1. Write your response to each statement (i.e., 1, 2, 3, 4, 5) in each of the blanks.
2. Add up the scores under each column. Place the result under each column.
3. Divide the subscale score by the number of statements in each column to get the average for each subscale.
4. Calculate the average for the whole inventory by adding up the subscale scores and dividing by 30.
5. Compare your results to those shown below.
6. Discuss your results with your teacher or tutor.

Global Reading Strategies (GLOB subscale)	Problem-Solving Strategies (PROB subscale)	Support Reading Strategies (SUP subscale)	Overall Reading Strategies
1. _____	8. _____	2. _____	GLOB _____
3. _____	11. _____	5. _____	PROB _____
4. _____	13. _____	6. _____	SUP _____
7. _____	16. _____	9. _____	
10. _____	18. _____	12. _____	
14. _____	21. _____	15. _____	
17. _____	27. _____	20. _____	
19. _____	30. _____	24. _____	
22. _____		28. _____	
23. _____			
25. _____			
26. _____			
29. _____			
_____ GLOB score	_____ PROB score	_____ SUP score	_____ Overall score
_____ GLOB mean	_____ PROB mean	_____ SUP mean	_____ Overall mean

Key to averages: 3.5 or higher = high   2.5–3.4 = medium   2.4 or lower = low

Interpreting your scores: The overall average indicates how often you use reading strategies when reading academic materials. The average for each subscale of the inventory shows which group of strategies (i.e., global, problem-solving, and support strategies) you use most when reading. With this information, you can tell if you score very high or very low in any of these strategy groups. Note, however, that the best possible use of these strategies depends on your reading ability in English, the type of material read, and your purpose for reading it. A low score on any of the subscales or parts of the inventory indicates that there may be some strategies in these parts that you might want to learn about and consider using when reading.

Summary

The teacher gathers data by asking questions that focus her evaluation of the strategies of the reader. First, she evaluates both oral and silent reading performance and determines the major presenting problem (print or meaning) using an informal reading inventory. Next, she evaluates the student's performance across levels of text difficulty using the informal reading inventory. From this information, she designates a level that is moderately difficult for the student. She decides whether print processing or meaning processing is inhibiting constructing meaning with text and establishes a level of performance. Then, she selects further assessments to expand knowledge of student's strategy use and skill development.

5

Selecting Instructional Techniques

Knowing *how* instruction occurs allows the teacher to modify his teaching effectively during the reading event. As he plans instruction, the teacher thinks about the techniques he uses and their influence on learning. By classifying techniques according to several critical characteristics, the teacher increases his specificity in matching instruction with the readers' patterns of constructing meaning. Therefore, this chapter classifies each teaching technique in the following ways:

1. The point at which the technique is implemented (before, during, or after)

2. The type of text being read (narrative or expository)

3. The mode of response (written or discussion)

4. The targeted reasoning strategy (prediction, monitoring, or elaboration)

5. The targeted reading skill (word identification, word analysis, fluency, meaning vocabulary, sentence comprehension, literal comprehension, or nonliteral comprehension)

6. The information source (reader-based or text-based)

7. The type of structure (explicit or implicit teaching)

The teacher selects a technique and analyzes its underlying characteristics. This analysis increases his effectiveness in implementing a particular technique and in broadening his knowledge of instructional alternatives. However, many teachers seem to be hesitant to change their routines even if they are not working well for individual students (Roskos & Walker, 1994). Another reason teachers resist change is a lack of knowledge about why one technique may be more effective in certain situations. This chapter and Part Two provide reasons why a given technique might be more effective under certain conditions. Knowledge about techniques allows teachers to make in-structional changes that facilitate student learning.

The instructional techniques, which are described in detail in Part Two, can be used either as a part of the guided reading lesson to support authen-tic reading activities or as part of a specific strategy or skill lesson to focus on areas of concern. The orchestration of the techniques depends on the strengths and needs of a particular reader.

The first major area lists techniques that demonstrate two characteristics. First, the techniques are analyzed by the point of instruction during guided contextual reading—before, during, or after reading takes place. Second, they are analyzed by mode of response—that is, whether the teacher encourages a written response or oral discussion. This table helps you identify techniques that will enhance learning during guided contextual reading. The teacher asks himself:

- At what point during the guided reading lesson will the student need support to construct the entire message?

- Can using more writing or discussion during the lesson build on the strengths of the learner?

The second area deals with the selection of techniques to encourage stu-dents' use of strategies and skills, and these techniques fit appropriately dur-ing the element of strategy and skill instruction (see Chapter 3). Here the teacher selects techniques that work on learner needs by showing students how to use their strengths when reading becomes difficult. To select appro-priate techniques for this part of the diagnostic teaching session, the teacher asks himself the following questions:

- Would a strategy that the student is not using be helpful to her? If so, how should I approach instruction so that she can use the new strat-egy in combination with the strategies she already uses?

- Does the student have a skill she is not using when she reads? If so, how should I mediate learning so that she incorporates this skill, us-ing her strengths?

The third area deals with the how to differentiate instruction. The diag-nostic teacher may need to identify specific procedures to use during instruc-tion. For instance, a reader might need a great deal of teacher direction. In this case, the teacher uses Table 5–5 on explicit instruction and narrows his previ-ous options, using this characteristic. To differentiate his selection of tech-niques, the teacher asks himself the following questions:

- If the student is overrelying on an information source, can I match this reliance with an instructional technique and show her how to integrate information sources?

■ What kind of teacher support does the student need? Does she need to work on her own or does she need more teacher direction?

Teaching techniques from different views of reading have been classified according to these key questions so that the teacher can match the students' strengths and needs and design lessons that mediate learning for each student.

Classifying Techniques for Guided Contextual Reading

When considering the instructional framework, the teacher thinks about the element of guided contextual reading and considers how instruction will occur as the student reads a particular selection so that the student constructs the meaning of the whole story. Selecting appropriate techniques facilitates a student's learning by providing instruction that assists the student when she can no longer learn independently. In other words, the instructional lesson is a planned exchange between independent student learning and teacher-guided learning. If the teacher intervenes with appropriate techniques, he can move the students to more complex reading strategies.

Classifying Techniques by Mode of Response

Readers' responses can be either oral or written. The teacher considers the students' interaction patterns by asking himself, "Will discussing or writing advance this student's reading? Which mode is this student's strength?" Whether the response is in written format or discussion format changes the task. Some students prefer to write about what they read, while others prefer to discuss what they read. Both processes are constructive and facilitate reading growth.

Writing and Reading

Writing and reading are supportive processes that can enhance each other. Writing about what was read facilitates reading. First, writing requires learners to reconstruct their understanding and thus prompts a more thoughtful response. The students can later use this written record of their thoughts to reflect on and analyze their thinking, and it allows the teacher to discuss students' interpretations with them. Writing brings inner thoughts into the open for verification and facilitates discussing personal interpretations.

Writing also facilitates reading because it reinforces the constructive process. Reading and writing require similar processes. Both readers and writers make plans about how they will construct meaning; both monitor their understandings to see whether they are making sense; both revise their thinking by rereading, using what was written and comparing it to what they know; both elaborate what was written, making connections between what was written and what is known to create new ideas. In these ways, both reading and writing are constructive processes in which one facilitates the other.

In addition, writing facilitates reading because both systems use the same writing conventions. Both use letters grouped together to form words, words grouped together to form sentences, and so on. The way the groups are formed follows certain patterns or conventions. Writing heightens students' awareness of how to use these conventions when they read. For instance, a young writer trying to spell *mother* thinks about how that word looked in the book *Are You My Mother?* Writing heightens an awareness of the visual features of words. It accomplishes the same task as flashing word cards. Writing facilitates reading through three avenues: reflective thinking, constructing meaning, and using written conventions.

Discussion and Reading

Discussing what students read does facilitate reading growth. When students verbalize their understanding of what they read, they reconstruct the text so that they can communicate their understanding to others. This constructive process is not simply a recall process. Readers think to themselves: "What is important and how do I communicate it to the others in the group? What did I learn that I want to share with this group? Did I think of something in a new light that would help others understand?" In fact, the meaning of students' interpretations has been found to change during the discussion. As students share their thinking, they co-construct meaning through social interaction. In ongoing discussions, meaning seems to be negotiated moment by moment as students rethink and discuss their understanding.

Social interaction facilitates reading, therefore, because it provides a vehicle for talking about the strategies, plans, and processes of meaning construction (Vygotsky, 1978). In other words, thinking about what is read is facilitated by conversations that encourage students to elaborate and explain their thinking. In this social situation, the teacher also explains and elaborates his thinking. This process allows the student to use tools, for thinking (words, plans, strategies, ideas, and so on). The teacher responds, encouraging a refinement of thinking (use of tools) and showing students how he constructs his answer.

This interaction facilitates students' independent use of literacy processes. As they discuss their thoughts and explain how they construct their answers, the new ideas and strategies they use become part of their internal thought processes. Through social interaction, students verbalize their thinking, discussing their strategies and their ideas. Thus, the verbalized strategies that come to the fore during discussion later become internal mental processes. During discussion, the teacher facilitates reading by discussing interpretations, asking students to justify their interpretations, and sharing his (the teacher's) own thought process. As a result, verbal discussion facilitates reading through three avenues: meaning construction, verbalizing plans and strategies for meaning construction, and making social thinking an internal process.

Conclusions About Mode of Response

The teacher thinks about the kind of responses the student makes. He asks, "Will this student profit from discussing or writing about what she reads?" He realizes that both processes facilitate meaning construction. Writing provides a written record of thoughts so that the student can reflect on how she constructs meaning, while verbal discussion allows the reader to revise ideas on the spot. The teacher selects a technique that matches the learner's strengths and needs. He thinks about the mode of response that the techniques demand and refers to Table 5–1 to select one that will assist the reader.

> Which mode of response (discussion or writing) will better assist this reader in advancing her reading?

Table 5–1 *Classifying Techniques by Mode of Response*

	Meaning Processing	
	Discussion	*Written Response*
Before	Collaborative Reading	Feature Analysis Grid
	Contextual Processing	Imagery Instruction
	Direct Experience Approach	K-W-L
	Experience-Text-Relationship	Webbing
	Webbing	
During	Directed Reading-Thinking Activity	Generative-Reciprocal Inference Procedure
	Guided Reading	Herringbone Technique
	Reciprocal Teaching	Prediction Logs
	ReQuest	Story Maps
	Say Something	
	Story Drama	
	Think-Aloud Approach	
After	Experience-Text-Relationship	Journal Writing
	Literature Circles	K-W-L
	Question-Answer Relationships	Opinion-Proof Approach
	Readers Theater	Question-Generation Strategy
	Retelling	Story Maps
	Story Drama	Story Writing Approach
		Summary Experience Approach
		Summarization
		Thematic Experience Approach

Classifying Techniques for Strategy and Skill Instruction

The second area is designed to help teachers select techniques that work on specific areas that are problematic for students. Although techniques can be used during either guided contextual reading or strategy and skill instruction, the purpose and focus of instruction are different (see Chapter 3). During guided contextual reading, the focus is on reading entire stories and understanding the content. The techniques are selected to enhance story understanding. However, during strategy and skill instruction, the teacher creates activities that focus on areas of concern. Because no one likes to focus on what one can't do, these lessons are short and use engaging passages. The minilessons focus on strategy deployment during reading. Rather than mastery, the teacher encourages the use of unfamiliar strategies and skills, showing students how to use their strengths in combination with their weaknesses. With each lesson, he strives to promote conversations about strategy and skill use. These conversations lead to discussion about how literacy works and how to use strengths to construct meaning with text.

During strategy and skill instruction, the teacher identifies students' strategy and skill needs and provides mediated instruction, showing students how a particular skill fits into their repertoire of reading strategies. In other words, the teacher creates an instructional context in which students can explore and talk about how strategies and skills are orchestrated. When selecting activities, the teacher must also remember that students might not use a particular strategy or skill as the result of a deficit. Instruction that begins with students' strengths is often more effective (see McCormick, 2003, for an elaboration of skill strengths and weaknesses).

For example, Student A uses background knowledge to identify unknown words; however, it is not always an effective strategy. She has a limited ability to manipulate the sounds of language (that is, she cannot segment sounds and then synthesize them to form words). In this case, the teacher helps the student develop a large sight vocabulary, using the impress method (see "Impress Method" in Part Two). It allows the student to bypass word analysis and use background knowledge and sentence comprehension to identify unknown words.

Although use of phonic knowledge would increase this student's reading performance, instruction in word analysis is futile unless the student can synthesize and segment sounds. As the student's reading fluency increases, the diagnostic teacher then encourages decoding by analogy, using this prompt: "What would make sense (strength) and sounds like another word you know (weakness)?" This latter instructional task is accomplished easily using repeated readings (see "Repeated Readings" in Part Two) with a discussion of strategy deployment.

In the preceding example, the teacher used the reader's strength to develop a successful reading program. Then he showed the student how to use her weaker skill area at times when using only her strength would not solve the reading problem. It is often necessary to try a variety of instructional techniques to find an appropriate one. For example, Student B is having difficulty with sight word identification. She is a bilingual student and has limited English language proficiency with no skill in sound synthesis. Typical techniques to develop sight word identification (word cards, language experience, and so on) prove futile until the new words are tied to a conceptual base. In this case, webbing (see "Webbing" in Part Two) is used to tie background knowledge to the sight words so that the student can associate what the words mean with how the words look.

The following sections elaborate the reasoning strategies and reading skills used during reading. The accompanying tables, Tables 5–2 (see p. 77) and 5–3 (see p. 82–83), identify instructional techniques for both reasoning strategies and skills.

Classifying Techniques by Reasoning Strategies

Readers strategically reason about what they are reading, applying skills when necessary. As students read, they select, sort, and evaluate the text against what they know. In essence, readers are involved in an active problem-solving process. They predict what is going to be communicated. Then they select and sort important information from the text and relate it to their prior knowledge. Next, they confirm or revise their predictions based on new textual information. Finally, they elaborate their understanding and strategy use. This reasoning process takes place automatically until readers cannot make sense of what they are reading. When readers encounter difficulty, they consciously employ a variety of monitoring strategies to reconstruct meaning. They actively work to regain meaning.

Although students exhibit individual variations in the strategies they employ, poor readers are not actively involved in constructing meaning. They view good reading as effortless; consequently, they do not make plans or vary their strategies as they read. Effective readers, however, are active. Before reading, "good readers use what they know about the topic, the type of text, the author's purposes and their own purposes to make predictions about the content of the text" (Duffy & Roehler, 1987, p. 416).

> Predicting requires guessing about what the author is going to say. It occurs before and during reading.

As they read, effective readers remain tentative and revise their predictions frequently, using a variety of reasons for their revisions. They intertwine the sources of information for revision (the text, background knowledge, or both) and the strategies for revisions (ignore the problem and read more, reread to check the facts, read ahead to clarify information, and consult an expert source). Effective readers stop, reflect, and flexibly shift between reader-based processing ("Does that make sense?") and text-based processing ("What did the text say?"). These actions are called monitoring reading.

> Monitoring requires checking the text or one's experience to see whether what one is reading is making sense. Monitoring occurs during reading.

Finally, effective readers fit new information into what they know by elaborating relationships among information. In other words, active readers automatically embellish text by drawing unstated inferences and picturing scenes and information as they read. These elaborations help them draw connections among ideas in the text and their own knowledge. Furthermore, as they elaborate textual information, they also generate new thoughts, creating new connections among ideas. Thus, elaboration is a generative process in which text prompts readers to enhance their thinking and expand their understanding.

> Elaborating requires relating new information to what is known in order to remember it. Thus, the new information becomes part of what is known. Elaborating occurs during and after reading.

Some readers, however, are less active. Their reading can break down in the predicting, monitoring, or elaborating phases of the reasoning process. Some readers do not use what they know to think about what the author might say. They read exactly what the text says without thinking about what it might mean. They need instruction that helps them make predictions about what the text will mean. Other readers venture a guess but hold on to the initial prediction even when the text does not support it. Some readers revise their predictions but change only one part of it, such as the *who, when, where,* or *how* information (Dybdahl & Walker, 1996). Some readers rely too heavily on the text or their background knowledge when monitoring their reading. They do not shift between knowledge sources to check their reading. These students need instruction in how to monitor their understanding of text. Other students fail to elaborate the relationship between what they know and the text; therefore, they cannot remember what they read. These readers need instruction in how to reason while they are reading.

Demonstrating reasoning strategies can improve the reading performance of poor readers. However, the teacher needs to evaluate the various instructional techniques. Some techniques lend themselves readily to talking about the different strategies of effective reading; others do not. Therefore, techniques have been classified here according to the reading strategy that they develop: predicting, monitoring, or elaborating. In addition, techniques can teach the reasoning process related to print processing or meaning processing. Table 5–2 classifies techniques for reasoning while processing print and meaning.

The teacher then looks for a strategy that, if learned, will improve this student's reading. He reflects on the strategies that the effective reader uses and evaluates how the student uses them. He returns to the data he has collected about the student's reading and looks at the hypotheses he formed when he analyzed the reading event. He considers whether the context or the text is affecting the strategies employed by this reader. If a strategy needs to be taught, the teacher uses Table 5–2, "Classifying Techniques by Reasoning Strategy," to identify techniques that facilitate learning the strategy. He asks the following question.

> Which strategy or strategies (predict, monitor, or elaborate), if learned, will increase this student's reading?

Classifying Techniques by Reading Skills

As readers strategically reason about what they are reading, they apply skills when necessary. Although meaningful interpretation of the text is the ultimate goal of reading instruction, certain tasks consume a major portion of children's thinking capacity as they develop as readers. The knowledge of particular skills is used as students reason about text; however, without the requisite skills knowledge, the reasoning process is hampered. The following explanation will provide a discussion first of the process of learning related to the overall reading task and then of the major skills involved at a given stage. Even though these skills have been associated with typical techniques, each skill can be developed through a variety of ways.

Stage One

For beginning readers, the major task is the association of oral language with its written equivalent. Young children have learned to communicate by using oral language within a social context. To read, however, they must infer the communicative intent of printed words. This new task places demands on learners. They must learn that printed words represent both a concept and spoken words. Therefore, the task of young readers is to develop this functional concept of printed language as well as the recognition of letters and sounds.

As these concepts of print develop, children begin to associate meaning with written words in stories. They automatically recognize a group of words at sight. They say, "I know a word that starts with *b* and is the same length, so this word must be *hat*." The development of a sight word vocabulary indicates that children are reasoning about the relationship between graphic symbols and meaning. Whether children use sounds, visual features,

Table 5–2   *Classifying Techniques by Reasoning Strategy*

	Print Processing	Meaning Processing
Prediction	Collaborative Reading Echo Reading Framed Rhyming Innovations Guided Reading Impress Method Language Experience Approach Shared Reading Sound Boxes Summary Experience Approach Talking Books	Cloze Instruction Directed Reading-Thinking Activity Graphic Organizers Experience-Text-Relationship Imagery Instruction K-W-L Listening-Thinking Activity ReQuest Think-Aloud Approach Thematic Experience Approach Directed Reading-Thinking Activity
Monitoring	Chunking Collaborative Reading Language Experience Approach Paired Reading Readers Theater Repeated Readings Shared Reading Word Walls	Generative-Reciprocal Inference Procedure Herringbone Technique Prediction Logs Reciprocal Teaching Story Maps Think-Aloud Approach Experience-Text-Relationship Herringbone Technique
Elaboration	Analytic Phonics Making Words Making and Writing Words Phonogram Approach Readers Theater Repeated Readings Retrospective Miscue Analysis Synthetic Phonics Word Analogy Strategy Word Probe Strategy Word Sorts	Journal Writing K-W-L Literature Circles Opinion-Proof Approach Question-Answer Relationships Question-Generation Strategy Reciprocal Teaching Retelling Story Drama Story Maps Summarization Thematic Experience Approach Vocabulary Self-Collection Strategy

Note: The techniques listed are the most effective; however, other techniques can be used. See individual techniques in Part Two.

or background knowledge, their major task is to develop this sight word knowledge, which generally consumes a major portion of their thinking through the middle of first-grade reading level.

TARGETED SKILLS FOR STAGE ONE

Word Identification

Based on
• Association of prior knowledge with printed words
• Ability to remember the visual form (visual memory)
• Ability to use the initial letter and word length to remember words

Typical techniques
• Language experience approach
• Shared reading approach

Stage Two

As students can read more words and longer stories, reading changes from a predominately oral, shared experience to silent reading and discussion. Thus, the reader begins to focus on text-based information, particularly on the patterns in words and stories. Because students can read longer stories, they encounter unfamiliar words that are not contained in their sight vocabularies. Therefore, emerging readers develop new ways to figure out unfamiliar words. In addition to experiential knowledge and sight word knowledge, they begin to use sound analogies to decode words (that is, "I know a sight word that looks similar to this new word; I will try substituting the sounds to see whether this new word makes sense in the story"). This stage of reading development is marked by the ability to use the alphabetic principle, namely, the understanding that words are made of sounds and letters that have a consistent pattern. Therefore, young readers match these patterns to known sight words.

As students begin to figure out many words independently, they can read longer stories; silent reading, therefore, becomes more efficient than oral reading. Thus, in order to communicate what they read, they retell the story, focusing on what the text said. This process places a high demand on literal comprehension because the learner's attention is focused on the logical development of a story line. Students begin to focus on the patterns of stories or how stories are organized (characters, problem, events, resolution) so that they can remember and retell more readily.

These skills occupy children's thinking capacity through the end of second grade, where techniques dealing with word analysis and literal comprehension are most appropriately employed.

TARGETED SKILLS FOR STAGE TWO

Word Analysis

Based on
- Ability to blend sounds (phonemic synthesis)
- Ability to divide words into their sounds (phonemic segmentation)
- Ability to use decoding analogies

Typical techniques
- Word analogy strategy
- Sound boxes

Literal Comprehension

Based on
- Understanding patterns in stories (story organization)
- Ability to determine what's important in the story to retell
- Use of background knowledge

Typical techniques
- Retelling
- Story maps

Stage Three

As learners encounter extended passages and chapter books where word meanings are embedded in complex sentence structures, the simple strategies of using known sight words, decoding by sound analogy, and thinking about the facts of a story are no longer sufficient. Because sentences are longer and more complex, students must focus on the forms of the sentences and match them with what they know about word and story meaning. This natural focus leads to increases in fluent word identification, which allows more thinking capacity for word, sentence, and idea meaning. Understanding sentence structure enhances fluent reading because the student breaks sentences into meaningful phrases and uses their background knowledge to predict sentence meaning. Sentence comprehension also enhances print processing because students must use sentence context as well as decoding by analogy. Using sentence context to figure out unknown words and simultaneously associating appropriate word meanings becomes a major task for these readers. This stage occupies students' thinking capacity through the middle of the fifth-grade reading level, where techniques developing fluency and sentence comprehension are most appropriately employed along with the students' continuing development of literal comprehension.

TARGETED SKILLS FOR STAGE THREE

Fluency

Based on

- Automatic association of how words look with what words mean
- Ability to break sentences into thought units
- Use of background knowledge to predict sentence meaning

Typical techniques

- Chunking method
- Readers theater

Sentence Comprehension

Based on

- Use of sentence structure to develop word meanings
- Use of sentence structure to decode words
- Prediction of sentence meaning to increase fluent reading

Typical techniques

- Cloze instruction
- Alternate writing

Stage Four

As students read more difficult text, they find the strategies that deal primarily with textual information are no longer sufficient. In texts at this level of difficulty, authors develop complex ideas that require an interpretation of text-based information within a reader's personal worldview. Therefore, readers must be able to strategically shift between text-based and reader-based processing, synthesizing their understanding. One important area of this stage is the increasing need to develop and use a meaning vocabulary, or definitional word knowledge. Readers at this stage must think about what each new word might mean and how it is like other words and ideas they already know. They must analyze what they know related to this new concept (word meaning) and integrate this knowledge with textbook usage. Likewise, they read for a variety of purposes and monitor their own understanding of text, questioning what is important to remember and how ideas and concepts fit together. This stage of development continues through the middle grades, where techniques emphasizing vocabulary knowledge and nonliteral comprehension are orchestrated with developing literal comprehension.

TARGETED SKILLS FOR STAGE FOUR

Meaning Vocabulary

Based on

- Integration of background knowledge with textual meaning
- Identification of likenesses and differences of word meanings
- Use of sentence and passage context to elaborate definitional knowledge

Typical techniques

- Webbing
- Contextual processing

Nonliteral Comprehension

Based on

- Synthesis of background knowledge with textual information
- Self-monitoring
- Self-questioning (I wonder what the author is going to say that is important to remember?)

Typical techniques

- Think-aloud approach
- Story drama

Thus, taking into account the appropriate stage for each reader, the teacher looks for a skill that, if learned, will increase this student's reading. He reflects on the major skills of reading and evaluates their influence on this reader's performance. He looks at the level of performance that is at the borderline range and matches it with the targeted skills for that reading level. Then he checks previous instructional experiences to evaluate their influence on the targeted skill. Basically, he asks; "Has this student received instruction in this skill and is still not proficient?" If a skill needs to be taught, the teacher uses Table 5–3, "Classifying Techniques by Reading Skills," to identify techniques that facilitate learning that skill.

Table 5–3   *Classifying Techniques by Reading Skills*

	Word Identification	Word Analysis	Fluency	Meaning Vocabulary	Sentence Comprehension	Literal Comprehension	Nonliteral Comprehension
Alternate Writing					*	*	*
Analytic (Implicit) Phonics		*					
Chunking			*		*		
Cloze Instruction				*	*	*	
Collaborative Reading	*		*				
Contextual Processing				*	*		
Directed Reading Activity	*			*		*	*
Directed Reading-Thinking Activity						*	*
Echo Reading	*		*		*		
Experience-Text-Relationship				*		*	*
Feature Analysis Grid				*			
Framed Rhyming Innovations		*		*	*		
Generative-Reciprocal Inference Procedure						*	*
Graphic Organizers						*	
Guided Reading	*		*			*	
Herringbone Technique						*	
Imagery Instruction						*	*
Impress Method	*		*				
Journal Writing							*
K-W-L						*	*
Language Experience Approach	*		*				
Literature Circles							*
Making Words	*	*					
Making and Writing Words	*	*		*			
Opinion-Proof Approach						*	*
Paired Reading	*		*				
Phonogram Approach		*					
Prediction Logs						*	*
Question-Answer Relationships						*	*

Table 5–3   *Continued*

	Word Identification	Word Analysis	Fluency	Meaning Vocabulary	Sentence Comprehension	Literal Comprehension	Nonliteral Comprehension
Question-Generation Strategy							*
Readers Theater			*			*	*
Reciprocal Teaching						*	*
Repeated Readings	*	*	*				
ReQuest						*	*
Retelling						*	*
Retrospective Miscue Analysis	*				*		
Say Something						*	*
Shared Reading Approach	*		*				
Sight Word Approach	*						
Sound Boxes		*					
Story Drama						*	*
Story Maps						*	*
Story Writing Approach					*	*	*
Summarization						*	*
Summary Experience Approach	*		*			*	
Synthetic (Explicit) Phonics		*					
Talking Books	*		*				
Thematic Experience Approach						*	*
Think-Aloud Approach						*	*
Vocabulary Self-Collection Strategy				*		*	*
Webbing				*		*	*
Word Analogy Strategy		*					
Word Probe Strategy		*					
Word Sorts	*	*					
Word Walls	*	*		*			

Note: (1) These classifications represent common uses for the techniques. Techniques can be adapted to accommodate the task demands of related skill areas; thus, word attack technique (synthetic phonics) might be used to establish a sight word vocabulary. (2) The lesson frameworks of strategy instruction, explicit teaching, implicit teaching, and sustained silent reading are not classified.

> Which skills, if learned, would increase this student's reading?

The instructional techniques in this book have been analyzed as to the major skill developed. The teacher checks the chart to identify how to work with skill needs.

Conclusions About Reading Strategies and Skills

After the teacher evaluates the student's reading level and formulates hypotheses about how the student reads, he plans the strategy and skill lessons. Using the data collected, the teacher identifies skills, strategies, or both that are inhibiting reading performance. He reviews the strategies employed by the reader as well as skill development. Then he selects an appropriate technique that will focus instruction on the targeted concern to improve the student's reading performance.

Classifying Techniques for Increased Specificity

The tables in this section are used in conjunction with the other tables. They increase the specificity of the previous selections. Readers demonstrate strengths and preferences that can be used to enhance active reading. Techniques that focus on critical areas for readers' progress are classified in this section in two ways: (1) by sources of information and (2) by type of structure.

Basically, reading is an interactive process in which readers use various sources of information (reader-based and text-based) at the same time to construct meaning with text. However, techniques differ according to which information sources are emphasized during instruction. Some techniques emphasize reader-based sources of information, while others stress text-based sources of information. Also, the type of structure needed during the lesson varies depending on the strengths and preferences of the reader. Some students profit from a structured, direct approach to the material, while other students prefer to structure their own learning and discover rules. Techniques differ in how they structure the learning task. These strengths can be matched with appropriate techniques, thus enhancing reading.

The techniques have been classified according to these characteristics, enabling the teacher to select techniques that match the students' strengths as he is teaching a new task. As the task is learned, he can select techniques that have a more integrative instructional approach. The teacher can thus use learner strengths to show students how to regain meaning when text interpretation breaks down. The following discussion and tables elaborate these areas.

Classifying Techniques by Sources of Information

Students vary the use of information sources as they read, depending on the situation and their purposes for reading. Because active-constructive reading depends on combining all available sources of information, readers use reader-based sources (topic knowledge, rhetorical knowledge, phonological knowledge, and so on) and text-based sources (letters, pictures, words, and so on) as needed to construct meaning.

Sometimes readers employ reader-based processes to predict what the text will say, using their own knowledge. These predictions frame the text-based processing and are subsequently confirmed or revised. The degree to which the reader engages in reader-based processing depends on her purposes for the task of reading. For example, one Saturday afternoon a young teen was reading a novel. As she read, she embellished the story making inferences from her own life, rapidly predicting what the characters would do next. In this instance, the young teen used a great deal of reader-based information as she read. However, at other times, readers choose to engage in text-based processing where they defer evaluation until they have read enough textual information to form a conclusion. This kind of processing occurs when readers encounter unfamiliar information, when their previous predictions have been disproved, when they read new directions, or when text fails to make sense. For example, on the next Saturday afternoon, this same young teenager was taking a college entrance examination. As she read the test directions, she read and reread the printed page, focusing on the information exactly as it was stated in the text. In this case, she used the text predominantly as an information source.

Effective readers perpetually shift between information sources to select, combine, and restructure data from the text and their personal knowledge. However, problem readers often experience a deficit in either a skill or strategy that causes them to shift away from one information source. They compensate by using their strength and thus eliminate a need to use their deficient knowledge source (Stanovich, 1986). Therefore, ineffective readers circumvent using their weaker information sources, and, as a result, often depend on a single source related to their strength.

Some readers have a wealth of general and topic knowledge, which they use continually to add to their general knowledge. They employ reader-based processes to predict what the text will say, using their topic knowledge and paying little attention to the text. This approach inhibits the development of knowledge sources dealing with the conventions of print. Because these readers overrely on reader-based processing of the content, they fail to develop knowledge sources dealing with the text. For example, Sandy entered first grade with poor phonemic awareness, as many potentially poor readers do (Juel, 1998). This weakness in a knowledge source inhibited her understanding of the phonetic system, which hindered her progress in the basal reader program that was used in the classroom. Therefore, Sandy used her strength of background knowledge to figure out words. When this strategy did not work, she made up the text by looking at the pictures. Thus, Sandy began to overrely on her reader-based strength, which inhibited her strategic meaning construction.

> Some readers overrely on reader-based information, making inferences from topic knowledge when a more careful reliance on the text is warranted.

Other readers, however, learn phonics easily and believe reading is accurately calling a string of words. When asked comprehension questions, they give answers using the exact words in the text even when inferences from topic knowledge are more appropriate. They have come to believe that meaning is found in the text. But as stories become more complex, they find that simply repeating sentences from the text does not result in understanding. For example, Dani rapidly reads words, seldom needing to monitor her understanding. This strategy seemed to work well when she read novels where the plot was similar to her own experiences. However, as she began reading content-area texts, she became lost. She could read the words, but she failed to check her understanding and elaborate new word meaning. Dani continued to passively read words and repeat text-based definitions (her strength) without relating ideas. This approach inhibited her development of strategic reading.

> Some readers overrely on text-based information, repeating text segments when inferences from background knowledge are more appropriate.

Instructional decision making is facilitated by knowing which information sources the reader is using and then matching those with particular techniques so that readers demonstrate their strength. After several successful reading experiences, the teacher chooses techniques that encourage strategically combining information sources. The techniques in this book have been classified by the source of information that is emphasized during instruction: (a) reader-based and (b) text-based. Some techniques initially ask students to use their prior knowledge, while other techniques ask students to use the information in the text.

Reader-Based Sources

When selecting approaches that focus on using reader-based information sources, the teacher identifies techniques that initially have the students use their background knowledge in relation to the content of the story. In using these techniques, the teacher continually asks students to think about what they know in order to create an expectation about what the text may say. For example, when using the directed reading-thinking activity (see Part Two), the teacher asks the students to predict what the story might be about. Then, after reading sections of the story, the teacher asks the students whether their predictions were on the right track or whether they would like to keep, add to, or change predictions. Thus, throughout the discussion, the teacher focuses on using reader-based inferencing to construct story understanding. Likewise, when the language experience approach is used (see Part Two), students are asked to tell a story, which is then recorded. This story constructed from the students' own words becomes the text, and the students are continually asked to refer to what they said (reader-based source) when they cannot figure out a word.

Text-Based Sources

When selecting approaches that focus on using text-based information sources, the teacher identifies techniques that initially ask students to use text-based information. In using these techniques, the teacher focuses on how the information in the text explains and describes major characters, events, and ideas. For example, in the story mapping approach (see Part Two), the teacher asks students to identify the setting (characters and place), the problem, the events that lead to the problem's resolution, and the resolution, and then write this information on a visual framework (map) for the story. The focus is on putting the text-based information on the story map. Likewise, when the synthetic phonics approach is used (see Part Two), students are asked to look closely at words and sound them out letter by letter. The students are continually asked to refer to the text when problems in print processing occur.

Conclusions About Sources of Information

Effective readers do not operate using either reader-based information or text-based information sources exclusively, but rather strategically combine these sources of information. What is necessary when reading is a flexible interplay between these sources. To help students develop more efficient use of both sources of information, the teacher begins by using the reader's strength (reader-based inferencing or text-based inferencing) and gradually introduces a merging of both sources of information by using scaffolding statements that prompt the student to combine sources. To expedite the selection of teaching techniques, Table 5–4 analyzes teaching techniques in terms of the major tasks and information sources. The teacher evaluates the students' use of information sources and analyzes the requisite task to be taught. He then selects a technique and constructs a lesson to verify the appropriateness of the technique.

> What source of information (text-based, reader-based, or both) does the student tend to use?

Table 5–4   *Classifying Techniques by Sources of Information*

	Reader-Based	Text-Based
Word Identification	Collaborative Reading Guided Reading Language Experience Approach Shared Reading Approach	Echo Reading* Impress Method* Sight Words
Word Analysis	Framed Rhyming Innovations Language Experience Approach Message Writing Making Words Making & Writing Words Sound Boxes Word Sorts	Analytic Phonics Phonogram Approach Synthetic Phonics Word Analogy Strategy Word Probe Strategy
Fluency	Chunking* Language Experience Paired Reading Readers Theater Summary Experience Approach	Cloze Instruction Echo Reading* Impress Method* Repeated Readings*
Vocabulary	Feature Analysis Grid* Vocabulary Self-Collection Strategy Webbing	Contextual Processing Cloze Instruction
Sentence Comprehension	Readers Theater Story Writing	Contextual Processing Cloze Instruction Framed Rhyming Innovations
Literal Comprehension	Experience-Text-Relationship Guided Reading K-W-L Retelling Say Something Story Writing Summary Experience Approach Webbing	Herringbone Technique Question-Answer Relationships Reciprocal Teaching ReQuest* Story Maps Summarization

Table 5–4   *Continued*

	Reader-Based	Text-Based
Nonliteral Comprehension	Experience-Text-Relationship Generative-Reciprocal Inference Procedure Imagery Instruction Journal Writing Literature Circles Opinion-Proof Approach* Prediction Logs Story Drama Think-Aloud Approach*	Question-Answer Relationships Reciprocal Teaching

*These techniques utilize both reader-based and text-based sources of information but focus slightly more on one or the other.

Note: The lesson frameworks of strategy instruction, explicit teaching, implicit teaching, directed reading activity, directed reading-thinking activity, and sustained silent reading are not classified.

Classifying Techniques by Type of Structure

Instructional decision making also includes an analysis of how mediated instruction will occur. The teacher thinks about how he will mediate learning. He asks what kind of structure (explicit or implicit) will be necessary for students to regulate their own learning. Learners differ in how they approach the reading event. Some readers are active, while others are passive.

Active Readers

Active readers are problem solvers. They select key characteristics by sampling several alternatives and flexibly shifting among sources of information. As they solve these problems, active readers use strategies for print and meaning processing. This may be an inherent way to process information, or it may be developed through the social interactions that students experience daily. Often the more active, independent learners have had numerous experiences with schoolbook language. To communicate socially, these students use a wide variety of words to describe events and elaborate descriptions to justify their actions. Through previous social interactions, they become more active and explicit when they solve verbal problems.

Passive Readers

Passive readers, however, learn by watching how other students and the teacher solve the problem. They have difficulty distinguishing between the context of learning (such as teacher praise and peer approval) and the task of learning. They approach problem solving as a spectator and remain passive toward their own process of learning, preferring to follow the teacher's model whenever possible. This passive stance may be an inherent way to process information, or it may be a result of the daily social interactions that the students experience.

Often the more passive students have relied on shared understandings during their social interactions. Communication is often limited to information that refers to events or ideas that are known to the listener; therefore, passive learners use less precise words and nonverbal language to communicate meaning. They rely on their listeners to infer meaning based on shared understandings rather than speaker explanations. When learning demands a more active verbal stance, these students are unfamiliar with the elaborate language that can be used to justify their actions. They remain passive, therefore, preferring to follow the teacher's model to solve problems.

Previous Experiences

For both active and passive students, previous experience with the task being taught affects the need for explicit instruction. If students have not had prior experiences related to the task, they might need some explicit instruction in the new task. If they have had prior experiences and *failed*, they might profit from explicit instruction that is different from the initial instructional context.

The teacher analyzes the students' need for explicit instruction by evaluating how active they are when solving the reading problem. If the students are active and have positive experiences with the task, the teacher chooses a task that focuses on implicit instruction (students read texts rich in language and figure out the underlying consistency as the teacher guides inquiry). However, if students are passive and have few positive experiences with the task, the teacher chooses a technique that focuses on explicit instruction (students are directly informed of what they are learning, provided a model, and given directed practice).

Explicit Instruction

In explicit instruction the teacher precisely states what is to be learned and models the thinking process that accompanies this new strategy or skill. Students are given reasons why this new strategy or skill will help them read better (Duke & Pearson, 2002). Minilessons are constructed to show them how to use the reading strategy or skill, with the teacher modeling the steps of the task. Guided practice with a high level of teacher feedback is then provided. The feedback explicitly explains when and where students would use the strategy or skill. In the explicit teaching model, however, a gradual release of teacher-directed instruction allows students to direct their own learning. The teacher identifies students who initially lack control of their own learning; then he explicitly teaches the new strategy. Finally, he plans for the independent use of the strategy.

EXPLICIT INSTRUCTION

Based on
- Reasons for learning
- Teacher modeling of how it works
- Collaborative practice
- Gradual release of teacher control

Typical techniques
- Word probe strategy
- Question-answer relationships

Implicit Instruction

Implicit instruction is characterized by an emphasis on the text, the reading event, and the student as informant. Large quantities of text are read, which require students to use the targeted strategy or skill. Students apply the strategy or skill to make sense of what is read without consciously understanding the principle. Because the context has been carefully arranged, students can readily decide which mistakes make a difference in understanding. From these choices, they reason about text interpretation. The teacher plays the role of linguistic inquirer, asking students, "How did you know that . . . ?" This role allows students to generate their own rules for text interpretation.

IMPLICIT INSTRUCTION

Based on
- Immersion in reading
- Teacher as linguistic inquirer
- Scaffolding thinking, using student responses
- Student generation of rules and ideas

Typical techniques
- Language experience
- Literature circles

Conclusions About Type of Structures

The teacher thinks about the student's reading performance and the information he has collected. He asks, "What kind of mediated instruction, implicit or explicit, will facilitate learning for this student?" In other words, does the student want direction on how to complete the tasks? Does she appear to need direct, explicit information before she attempts a reading task or does she want to control her own learning? The teacher theorizes about the kind of mediated instruction the student needs in order to change her reading behavior. The teacher predicts whether implicit (student-discovered strategies) or explicit (teacher-directed learning) instruction will result in a greater change in reading performance. The teacher matches this hypothesis with an appropriate technique using Table 5–5.

> In order to advance reading, what kind of mediated instruction (implicit or explicit) will be needed?

Table 5–5   *Classifying Techniques by Type of Structure*

	Implicit	*Explicit*
Word Identification	Collaborative Reading Echo Reading Impress Method Language Experience Approach Listening-Thinking Activity Shared Reading Approach Summary Experience Approach Talking Books	Multisensory Approaches Sight Word Approach Word Walls
Word Analysis	Analytic Phonics Making Words Making & Writing Words Repeated Readings Sound Boxes Word Sorts	Framed Rhyming Innovations Phonogram Approach Synthetic Phonics Word Analogy Strategy Word Probe Strategy
Fluency	Echo Reading Impress Method Language Experience Approach Paired Reading Readers Theater Talking Books	Chunking Repeated Readings (with teacher mediation)
Meaning Vocabulary	Cloze Instruction Thematic Experience Approach Vocabulary Self-Collection Strategy Webbing	Contextual Processing Experience-Text-Relationship Word Walls

Table 5–5 *Continued*

	Implicit	*Explicit*
Sentence Comprehension	Alternate Writing Cloze Instruction Retrospective Miscue Analysis Story Writing	Contextual Processing Framed Rhyming Innovations
Literal Comprehension	Alternate Writing K-W-L Readers Theater ReQuest Retelling Say Something Story Writing	Herringbone Technique Opinion-Proof Approach Reciprocal Teaching Story Maps Summarization
Nonliteral Comprehension	Imagery Instruction Journal Writing Literature Circles Prediction Logs Readers Theater Story Drama	Experience-Text-Relationship Generative-Reciprocal Inference Procedure Think-Aloud Approach

Note: (1) The lesson frameworks of strategy instruction, explicit teaching, implicit teaching, directed reading activity, directed reading-thinking activity, and sustained silent reading are not classified. Of these, explicit teaching and the directed reading activity are explicit techniques. (2) Teacher implementation can change any technique to make it more or less explicit or implicit.

▮ Summary

The teacher's selection of a technique reflects the hypotheses about a student's learning at that particular time. To select the most appropriate technique, the teacher analyzes each technique according to its instructional features. First, the teacher thinks about the instructional framework during guided contextual reading and selects techniques that will lead the student to interpret whole stories meaningfully. He thinks about students' preferences and decides whether more writing or discussing will advance story understanding.

Next, the teacher selects techniques to encourage students to use areas of concern. He thinks about the element of strategy and skill instruction and selects techniques that work on concerns by showing students how to use their strengths to support their weaknesses.

Finally, the teacher refines his selections by checking the selection against students' strengths and needs so he can use these during instruction. He uses as criteria source of information and type of mediated instruction. He thinks about the sources of information on which students rely: reader-based or text-based. He matches this assessment with instructional techniques that show them how to integrate information sources while at the same time use their strength. Then he decides on the type of structure that is needed: explicit or implicit. Providing the appropriate type of mediated instruction in the learning situation enhances students' reading performance.

Throughout his instruction, the teacher makes instructional modifications that increase each student's reading performance. To date, no single instructional sequence or instructional framework has proven effective for problem readers. However, teachers vary in their preferences for teaching, and these preferences often dictate how they conduct reading lessons. Effective teachers remember that student learning is not accomplished by a mindless implementation of instructional techniques, but by understanding the variables in the process of reading. Therefore, the teacher needs to employ a variety of techniques to meet the individual needs of readers, identify the key features of these techniques, and evaluate how these features affect reading acquisition.

PART TWO

Instructional Techniques

In this part, 55 instructional procedures are presented to help teachers design programs for reading instruction. The instructional procedures, or techniques, include a variety of instructional formats, approaches, methods, and specialized techniques. The techniques represent a variety of ways to encourage proficient reading. Each technique is discussed in two parts: (a) a simple procedural description followed by (b) an explanation of specific diagnostic applications.

When teaching, this part may be used in the following manner. First, the teacher consults the general description and its steps. To make instructional modifications, the teacher needs to evaluate how she instructs the lesson. As she instructs the lesson, she evaluates at what point she modified instruction to mediate learning. Consequently, this part describes the steps in implementing each technique, thus facilitating a comparison of how instruction occurs when using various techniques. The teacher may then wish to turn to the second section of the discussion; the knowledge of learner patterns in which the technique produces success. This will be of assistance when the teacher tries to match an instructional technique to the strength and needs of a student.

The Information for Each Technique

Initially, the explanation is presented in simple terminology and is constructed to assist teacher-parent collaboration. The following topics are included:

- *Description.* In an effort to simplify communication, a two- or three-sentence description is presented. This description can be used in report writing or communicating with parents.

- *Targeted Reading Levels.* Many techniques were developed for use with students at a particular stage in reading development. This section will facilitate selecting a technique that matches the reading level of the student.

- *Predominant Focus of Instruction.* This section delineates the critical focus of each technique. Techniques can be placed on a continuum of various instructional features that are stressed during implementation. For example, most techniques have both an oral discussion and a written component; however, one of these aspects will predominate. It must be remembered that the significance of this emphasis depends on the learner's strategies, his task knowledge, and the situational context. The following list represents the various foci:

  1. Print or meaning processing
  2. Instructional phase (before, during, or after reading) in the lesson
  3. Response mode emphasized (oral or written)
  4. Strategy emphasized (prediction, monitoring, or elaboration)
  5. Skill emphasized (word identification, word analysis, fluency, sentence comprehension, word meaning, literal comprehension, or nonliteral comprehension)
  6. Source of information (text-based or reader-based)
  7. Type of instruction (explicit or implicit)

- *Procedures.* This section is a sequential enumeration of the process of instruction for each technique. This explanation serves two purposes. First, it facilitates implementation of the technique so that experimenting with new methods of instruction is not overwhelming. Second, using the steps of instruction, the teacher can analyze in what part of the instruction the student has incorporated the desired reading behaviors. This knowledge facilitates modifying instruction to increase its effectiveness.

The next section specifies the applications of each technique and includes the following elements:

- *Basic View of Reading.* Techniques have developed from various views of learning. As individuals formulate views of how learning occurs in young children, they propose teaching techniques that support their views. Therefore, instructional techniques reflect theories about how children learn. An assumption of this part is that the teacher can match how a child is learning with a technique that reflects that learning process. The major views are text-based, which focuses instruction on text-based processing; reader-based, in which instruction is focused on reader-based processing; interactive, with instruction focused on combining reader-based and text-based processing; and socio-interactive, in which instruction is focused on shared meaning construction (see Chapter 1).

- *Patterns of Strengths and Strategies*. This section looks specifically at what the student is asked to do when the teacher implements the technique. The underlying strengths and strategies that are necessary for the student to profit from this instructional technique are then presented.

- *Learner Patterns That Produce Increased Engagement*. Techniques can be used in different ways to engage students in literacy. This section analyzes the technique as it would be integrated into instruction with different learners. Learner patterns (see Chapter 5 for further explanation) that are highlighted in this section include the following:

  1. *Active readers*, who independently solve reading problems by reorganizing new information around its key features. They predict, monitor, and elaborate what they read, using both the text and what they know.
  2. *Passive readers*, who rely heavily on cues from their environment to decide what is important to remember. They prefer to follow a teacher's model when predicting, monitoring, and elaborating what they read. When reading, they use either the text or what they know to solve the reading problem.

Described first are the learner patterns that represent how the technique matches a learner strength. The items designated by an asterisk, which appear second, represent how the technique would be used to remediate a weakness during strategy and skill instruction.

Alternate Writing

Description   Alternate writing is the composition of a story among a group of students and a teacher. Writing for a specified amount of time, each person alternately continues the development of a cohesive story line. Each person's contribution to the story line must build upon prior information in the composition and must lead to the next event.

Text   Students' and teacher's writing

Predominant Focus of Instruction

1. Processing focus: meaning
2. Instructional phase: during reading
3. Response mode emphasized: written discourse
4. Strategy emphasized: elaboration
5. Skill emphasized: sentence comprehension
6. Source of information: reader-based
7. Type of instruction: implicit

Procedure

1. The teacher selects topics of interest to the students. As the procedure is used, an increasing variety of text types and subject areas needs to be included.
2. Using the story starter or topic selected, the teacher begins writing and continues developing the story line for 2 minutes. In a small group, an overhead can be used.
3. The story is passed to the next student. This student writes for 2 minutes.
4. In order to continue the story, each student must read the previous text and create text that maintains the story theme and moves the story to its conclusion.
5. When the story is completely written, the teacher reads the story as a whole.
6. The teacher revises her own parts of the story for coherence and grammatical clarity. As she is revising, she thinks out loud, "Will this make sense to my reader?"
7. The teacher encourages students to revise their writing for coherence and grammatical clarity.

Modifications

1. A story map can be developed prior to writing so that each student adds information that will fit the story map (see "Story Map" in this part).
2. A word processing program can be used, and students can write and revise the story on the computer.
3. Cartoons can be used as a framework for the story line.
4. This technique can be used in pairs, small groups, and tutoring situations.
5. This technique can be easily adapted to a writing center, where students add to the story when they attend that center. Students initial their additions.

Further Applications

Basic View of Reading   Reading and writing are socio-interactive processes in which the reader's ideas are shaped by group members. He uses prior knowledge to construct and monitor understanding, asking himself what would fit the story and be meaningful to group members. Through writing, the reader becomes sensitive to how stories are constructed so that they make sense.

Patterns of Strengths and Strategies   Alternate writing is most appropriate for students who prefer to communicate through writing rather than discussing. This approach helps students develop a sense of the story line and approach text as a communication between reader and writer.

Learner Patterns That Produce Increased Engagement

1. For the learner who writes well but does not understand that reading is a communication process, this technique provides a tool for talking about the communicative intent of the author.
2. For the learner who writes and reads for self-understanding and meaning but does not realize that the text is a contractual agreement between reader and writer, this technique provides a tool for talking about what needs to be in a text to make it understandable to a reader.
*3. For a learner who has verbal difficulty and who needs to participate in writing a story to understand story structure, this technique provides an experience in developing writing fluency in a group setting, which is less threatening.

For Further Reading

Short, K. G., Harste, J C., & Burke, C. (1996). *Creating classrooms for authors and inquirers*. Portsmouth, NH: Heinemann.

---

*Indicates a technique that can be used to remediate a weakness.

■ Analytic (Implicit) Phonics   *Targeted Reading Levels 1–2*

Description   Analytic phonics (sometimes referred to as implicit phonics instruction) is an approach to teaching decoding that is based on drawing phonic relationships among words that have the same letter patterns. Using words already recognized "at sight," the student identifies the sounds of letter groups by making analogies to known words. In other words, the child says, "I already know a word that looks like this new word. I will match the sounds in that word with the sounds in the new word."

Text   Known sight words and new words that have the same sound pattern

Predominant Focus of Instruction

1. Processing focus: print
2. Instructional phase: after reading
3. Response mode emphasized: oral discussion
4. Strategy emphasized: elaboration
5. Skill emphasized: word analysis
6. Source of information: text-based
7. Type of instruction: implicit

Procedure

1. The teacher selects a text that contains an abundance of the letter sounds to be taught.
2. The teacher presents sight words that represent the targeted sound or sound cluster. For example, she places these words on the board: *green grass grow*
3. She asks the student to identify how these words are alike. The student responds, "They all have the letters *gr* at the beginning."
4. The teacher directs attention to the sounds by saying, "How does the *gr* sound in these words?"
5. If the student cannot figure out the sound, the teacher says, "Try the *gr-r-r* sound as in *green, grass,* and *grow.*"
6. The student reads a text with words that have the *gr* sound, such as the following:

   In the land of the gremlins, there were gobs of green grapes as big as Grandpa. One baby gremlin loved to eat the green grapes. He began to grow and grow and grow. So his mother said, "You cannot eat anymore. You have grown too big." This made the gremlin grumpy. He growled and growled. He grabbed a great big green grape and gobbled it up. Then he grabbed another green grape and globbled it up. Then he grabbed another and another and another. He grew and grew and grew until he popped. That was the end of the gremlin.

7. The teacher draws attention to how the student used the letter clusters to figure out the words.

Further Applications

Basic View of Reading   Learning to read is a text-based process in which the learner makes inferences about the phonic relationships within words. When a student can read an abundance of words that contain a consistent phonic relationship, he will infer the phonic rule for the target words and similar words. This process is called *implicit* or *analytic phonics.*

Patterns of Strengths and Strategies   Analytic phonics is most appropriate for students who can segment words into their sounds and readily make phonic inferences about the consistency of sounds in words. This technique builds on their strengths and allows them to develop the strategy of decoding.

Learner Patterns That Produce Increased Engagement

1. For a learner who can segment words into their sounds and has established a sight word vocabulary, this technique matches his strengths in knowing the whole word before the parts and finding the patterns between what he knows and what is new.
2. For an active reader who does not respond to the direct instruction of other decoding approaches, this technique allows him to develop his own rules for how phonics works.
3. For a learner who has an overriding need for meaning and purpose in his learning, minimal instruction in decoding makes sense and provides strategies for decoding.

For Further Reading

McCormick, S. (2003). *Instructing students who have literacy problems* (4th ed.). Upper Saddle River, NJ: Merrill/Prentice Hall.

Snow, C. E., Burn, M. S., & Griffin, P. (1998). *Preventing reading difficulties in young children.* Washington, DC: National Academy Press.

■ *Chunking* *Targeted Reading Levels 4–8*

Description   Chunking is a technique to encourage the student to read phrases of language that represent meaning rather than separate words. It focuses on reading phrases of text that represent a thought. Chunking facilitates comprehension and fluency by using thought units rather than word-by-word reading.

Text   All kinds

Predominant Focus of Instruction

1. Processing focus: print and meaning
2. Instructional phase: during reading
3. Response mode emphasized: oral production
4. Strategy emphasized: prediction
5. Skill emphasized: fluency and sentence comprehension
6. Source of information: text-based and reader-based
7. Type of instruction: explicit

Procedure

1. The teacher chooses a passage at an instructional reading level that will take about 3 minutes to read.
2. The teacher tapes the student reading the passage.
3. The teacher and the student echo read (see "Echo Reading" in this part) the passage using meaningful phrases. In other words, the teacher reads a sentence modeling appropriate chunks of the sentence, and the student repeats the same sentence using the phrasing. The example that follows illustrates the sequence:

   Text: The bright girl liked to read stories about horses.

   Student reading: The/bright/girl/liked/to/read/stories/about/horses.

   Teacher modeling: The bright girl/liked to read/stories about horses.

   Student echoing: The bright girl/liked to/read stories/about horses.

   Teacher comment: I liked the way you chunked "read stories." Did it make more sense to you to read it that way?

4. The teacher and student continue reading the entire passage. When possible, the teacher increases the number of sentences chunked before the student repeats the model.
5. As the student's ability to chunk thought units increases, the teacher ceases to model the chunking, and the student reads the passage on her own.
6. The teacher tapes the reading of the passage again.
7. The teacher and the student compare fluency, intonation, and phrasing.

Modifications

1. For the extremely slow reader, the teacher may incorporate oral chunking experiences as an intervention with multiple timed, silent readings.
2. For the beginning reader, chunking a language experience story by writing phrases from the story on 3″ × 5″ cards is an effective technique.

Further Applications

Basic View of Reading   Reading is an interactive process whereby a reader thinks about how the words of the text are combined to form the ideas the author intended to convey.

Patterns of Strengths and Strategies   Chunking is most appropriate for students who have facility with word identification and reflect a sequential, text-based processing. Chunking of text encourages these students to connect the underlying thought with the text as they are reading.

Learner Patterns That Produce Increased Engagement

*1. When chunking, a learner who has difficulty relating what is written in the text to his own thoughts must use understanding of the meaning to group the words together.
*2. For the passive reader who reads words without thinking of their meaning, chunking uses recognizing the words (a strength) to understand how the words create meaning (a weakness).
*3. For a learner who is word-bound because of an overemphasis on phonics or oral accuracy, chunking increases her fluency and speed.
*4. For an extremely slow reader who thinks about every word, chunking encourages thinking about groups of words rather than individual words.

For Further Reading

Rasinski, T., & Padak, N. (2001). *From phonics to fluency.* Upper Saddle River, NJ: Merrill/ Prentice Hall.

■ Cloze Instruction   *Targeted Reading Levels 4–12*

Description   The instructional cloze is a technique that develops comprehension by deleting target words from a text. It encourages the student to think about what word would make sense in the sentence and in the context of the entire story.

Text   Paragraphs and stories that are coherent

Predominant Focus of Instruction

1. Processing focus: meaning
2. Instructional phase: after reading
3. Response mode emphasized: written
4. Strategy emphasized: prediction and monitoring
5. Skill emphasized: sentence comprehension and word meaning
6. Source of information: text-based with some reader-based
7. Type of instruction: implicit

Procedure

1. The teacher selects a text of 200–400 words.
2. The teacher decides on the target words, such as nouns or verbs or targeted sight words.
3. The teacher systematically deletes the words from the paragraph and inserts a blank for the deleted word.
4. The student is instructed to read the entire passage to get a sense of the entire meaning.
5. The student is then instructed to fill in the blanks in the passage.
6. When the student finishes filling in the blanks, the answers are evaluated as to the similarity of meaning between the deleted word and the supplied word.
7. The student reviews his choices and talks about what strategies he used to decide on the word choices.

Modifications

1. An oral cloze can be used to develop predictive listening in the young child.
2. A cloze exercise can be constructed from language experience stories in order to develop the ability to predict a word by using prior knowledge (what I said) and the text (how I said it).
3. Cloze can be adapted so that pairs of students work together to decide what word fits in the text. This activity causes a discussion and justification of word choices.

Further Applications

Basic View of Reading   Reading is an interactive process of verifying text expectation by using knowledge of how language works (sentence structure) and what the passage means (overall contextual meaning).

Patterns of Strengths and Strategies   The cloze procedure relies on a well-developed sense of the redundancy of language and a manipulation of sentence structure. For students who have verbal fluency, this technique facilitates comprehension by encouraging the combination of text and meaning cues.

Learner Patterns That Produce Increased Engagement

*1. For the learner who has become word-bound during the process of initial reading instruction and needs to increase the use of context to construct meaning, this technique increases the ability to guess what words are from context.
*2. For the learner who tends to read isolated words rather than using the context and asking what would make sense, this technique helps the reader think about what groups of words mean.
*3. For the learner who needs to use both sentence structure and overall meaning to read text effectively, this technique focuses attention on sentence meaning.

For Further Reading

Reutzel, D. R., & Cooter, R. B. (2003). *Strategies for reading assessment and instruction: Helping every child succeed* (2nd ed.). Upper Saddle River, NJ: Merrill/Prentice Hall.

■ Collaborative Reading   *Targeted Reading Levels 2–5*

Description   In the collaborative reading technique, the challenge of unfamiliar selections is supported by reading together and sharing interpretations as with young children in shared reading. The teacher begins reading the story aloud and then invites the student to follow. They discuss what the story could be about as they read the story to develop an understanding of the story while reading together. Using his understanding of the story, the student reads the new selection on his own with only minimal support from the teacher.

Text   Easy chapter books

Predominant Focus of Instruction

1. Processing focus: meaning and print
2. Instructional phase: before reading
3. Response mode emphasized: oral discussion
4. Strategy emphasized: prediction
5. Skill emphasized: literal comprehension and word identification
6. Source of information: reader-based
7. Type of instruction: implicit

Procedure

1. The teacher selects chapter book to read.
2. The teacher and students discuss what they think the book will be about based on the title.
3. The teacher reads the story aloud modeling appropriate intonation. (If the student is reading well, then the first read is not necessary, but the teacher can ask the following questions as she and the student read together.) As the teacher reads, she stops and asks

   What do you think will happen next?

   Do you agree with what the main character did?

4. After the first reading the teacher asks open-ended questions that encourage a higher level of engagement in the selection, such as

   Which part of the story did you like best?

   What would you change in the story?

5. When reading the story a second time together, the teacher keeps a fluent pace and invites the student to join in the reading.
6. After the second reading, the student and teacher review the troublesome phrases and ideas.
7. On the third reading of the story, the student reads alone. The teacher prompts the student if he needs help.

Further Applications

Basic View of Reading Reading is a socio-interactive process in which the reader's background knowledge and how he discusses the story with others help him understand the story and recognize the words. When the teacher reads the story aloud and discusses it with the child, she creates an expectation for the words in the text. The student then uses reader-based processing (i.e., what the text means) to figure out unfamiliar words. The ultimate goal is a reader who will simultaneously apply the decoding skills of reading while comprehending text.

Patterns of Strengths and Strategies Collaborative reading is most appropriate for intermediate students who have a high drive for meaning when reading. For these students, the approach uses their strengths of listening and thinking; then it asks them to use these strengths to recognize words.

Learner Patterns That Produce Increased Engagement

1. For a learner with a high listening comprehension and minimal (second-grade) word identification skills, this technique uses his strength in listening and thinking to develop an anticipation of what the text will say and facilitates word identification.
*2. For a passive learner with adequate listening comprehension skills and minimal word identification skills, the teacher needs to emphasize self-talk when revising miscues.
*3. For an extremely word-bound reader who lacks fluency, this technique uses what the student hears to develop expectations for what words will be in the text.

For Further Reading
Rasinski, T., & Padak, N. (2004). *Effective reading strategies: Teaching children who find reading difficult* (3rd ed.). Upper Saddle River, NJ: Merrill/Prentice Hall.

■ Contextual Processing   *Targeted Reading Levels 2–12*

Description   Contextual processing is a technique used to develop new word meanings as they are found in the context of a selected story. This technique shows the student how to use context to figure out what new vocabulary words mean.

Text   Paragraphs three to four sentences long, where the meaning of new vocabulary is apparent from the surrounding context

Predominant Focus of Instruction

1. Processing focus: meaning
2. Instructional phase: before or after reading
3. Response mode emphasized: oral discussion
4. Strategy emphasized: monitoring and elaboration
5. Skill emphasized: word meaning and sentence comprehension
6. Source of information: text-based
7. Type of instruction: explicit when using modification

Procedure

1. The teacher selects unfamiliar key vocabulary words to teach.
2. The teacher finds a passage in the text where the meaning of the word is apparent from the surrounding context. If such texts are not available, she creates her own three-sentence paragraph.
3. She writes the paragraph on the overhead or chalkboard.
4. She reads the paragraph aloud to the students.
5. The students reread the paragraph silently.
6. The teacher asks the students about the meaning of the word found in the paragraph, asking, for example, "What does the paragraph tell you about the word . . . ?"
7. The teacher uses the students' answers to probe further understanding, asking, "Why did you think that?"
8. The teacher asks students to write down what the new word might mean.
9. The teacher has students think of other similar situations in which they could use the word. She asks, "Who else might be . . . ? Where else might you . . . ?"
10. The students think of other words with similar meanings.
11. The students record target words and a personal definition in their vocabulary journals.

Modification   The teacher can increase the explicitness of the technique by modeling how to figure out the meaning of the word using the surrounding words in the paragraph. The teacher models step 6 (what the paragraph told her), step 7 (why she thought that), and step 8 (how she came up with the meaning).

Further Applications

Basic View of Reading   Reading is an interactive process in which the readers use what they know about the words in the story to elaborate word meaning.

Patterns of Strengths and Strategies   Contextual processing has students figure out unfamiliar word meanings from the context; therefore, it is most appropriate for students who have facility with sentence meaning but do not use this strategy to figure out what new words mean. This pattern is commonly used by strategy learners who have facility with sentence structure but do not combine this with what they already know to expand their understanding of word meanings.

Learner Patterns That Produce Increased Engagement

1. For a learner who has the ability to use sentences to figure out how to pronounce new words but does not use his sentence knowledge to expand word meanings, this technique starts with his strength and then asks him to use sentence knowledge and background knowledge to elaborate word meaning.
*2. For a passive learner who reads the words without actively thinking about what they mean in the new context or other contexts, this technique encourages him to think actively about what words mean. The modification of modeling may be needed.
*3. For a learner who does not use the sentence context to figure out word meanings, this technique encourages him to use context as well as what he knows to figure out new word meanings.

For Further Reading

Gipe, J. P. (2002). *Multiple paths to literacy: Classroom techniques for struggling readers* (5th ed.). Upper Saddle River, NJ: Merrill/Prentice Hall.

Gunning, T. G. (1998). *Assessing and correcting reading and writing difficulties*. Boston: Allyn & Bacon.

■ *Directed Reading Activity*   *Targeted Reading Levels: All levels*

Description   A directed reading activity (DRA) is an instructional format for teaching reading in which the teacher assumes the major instructional role. The teacher develops background knowledge, introduces new words, and gives the students a purpose for reading. Then she directs the discussion with questions to develop reading comprehension. Finally, she reinforces and extends the skills and knowledge developed in the story.

Text   Graded stories in basal readers or content-area textbooks

Predominant Focus of Instruction

1. Processing focus: print and meaning
2. Instructional phase: before and after reading
3. Response mode emphasized: oral discussion
4. Strategy emphasized: elaboration
5. Skill emphasized: word identification and literal comprehension
6. Source of information: text-based
7. Type of instruction: implicit

Procedure

1. The teacher develops readiness for reading:
   a. The teacher presents new vocabulary words in oral and written context. Students are asked what these new words mean and directed to remember the words by their distinctive visual features.
   b. The teacher develops appropriate background knowledge so that students will understand the general setting of the story.
   c. The teacher gives the students a purpose for reading by telling them to read to find out a particular thing or concept. She develops purposes that require students to read the entire story before an answer is resolved.
2. The students read the story silently.
   a. If necessary, the teacher divides the story into sections. After the students read a section, the teacher asks a variety of questions emphasizing literal and nonliteral story understanding.
   b. The teacher asks the students to support their answers by reading aloud the appropriate sections in the text.
3. The teacher reinforces and extends concepts introduced in the story.
   a. Activities to reinforce word recognition and word meanings are used to develop independence in reading.
   b. Activities that develop a creative response to the story are assigned.
   c. Activities that require students to relate the story to their own experiences and to other stories are used.

Further Applications

Basic View of Reading   Reading requires recognizing words and then associating meaning with these new words. Initially, therefore, reading is a text-based process. However, when new words have been learned and purposes have been set, students can read with comprehension.

Patterns of Strengths and Strategies   A directed reading activity is a flexible approach for instructing children to read. Following this format, the text can be narrative or expository short or long, interrupted or read as a whole. However, remember that the directed reading activity is just that, reading directed by the teacher and not the student. Therefore, it is most appropriate when a substantial amount of teacher direction is needed to construct meaning.

Learner Patterns That Produce Increased Engagement

1. For the active reader who needs new words presented before he reads so that word recognition does not interfere with story comprehension, this approach introduces new words to facilitate story comprehension.
*2. For the reader who needs the teacher to direct his attention to important word recognition and comprehension cues, the teacher can begin with this format but should phase as quickly as possible to strategies that require a more active stance from the reader.

For Further Reading

Gunning, T. G. (1998). *Assessing and correcting reading and writing difficulties.* Boston: Allyn & Bacon.

Tierney. R. J., & Readence, J. E. (2005). *Reading strategies and practices: A compendium* (6th ed.). Boston: Allyn & Bacon.

Directed Reading-Thinking Activity

Targeted Reading Levels: All levels

Description A directed reading-thinking activity (DRTA) is an instructional format for teaching reading that includes predicting what the author will say, reading to confirm or revise those predictions, and elaborating responses. Teachers and students discuss both strategies and responses.

Text Can be applied to all narrative and expository texts

Predominant Focus of Instruction

1. Processing focus: meaning
2. Instructional phase: during and after reading
3. Response mode emphasized: oral discussion
4. Strategy emphasized: prediction and monitoring
5. Skill emphasized: nonliteral comprehension
6. Source of information: reader-based and text-based
7. Type of instruction: implicit

Procedure

1. The teacher asks students to predict what will happen in the story by using the title and any available pictures.
2. She continues her questioning by asking students why they made their predictions.
3. The students read to a turning point in the story.
4. The teacher asks students whether their predictions were confirmed.
5. The teacher asks students to support their answers, using the information in the text, and explain their reasoning.
6. The teacher then asks the following questions:

   *What do you think is going to happen next?

   *Why do you think that?

7. The students read to the next turning point in the story.
8. The teacher repeats steps 4, 5, 6, and 7.
9. When they are finished reading, the teacher and students react to the story as a whole.
10. The teacher leads students to analyze the story in relation to other stories, personal experiences, and the author's purpose.
11. The teacher discusses the strategies that were used to understand the story.
12. The teacher reviews the meaning of any key vocabulary words.

Further Applications

Basic View of Reading Reading is an active thinking process in which a reader predicts, confirms, and revises his interpretation, using important textual information. The reflective thought process focuses on not only what was understood about the story but also how it was understood.

Patterns of Strengths and Strategies A DRTA is appropriate for students who readily engage in constructing meaning as they read. They use what they already know to predict what will happen in the story and then select important information from the text to justify their answers. The teacher matches these active strategies by discussing not only what students think but also how they think.

Learner Patterns That Produce Increased Engagement

1. For the active reader who uses what he already knows and the text to construct meaning, a DRTA allows this reader to construct meaning with the guidance of the teacher.
*2. For the reader who uses what he already knows to understand stories but has difficulty justifying his answers with information from the text, this technique requires the reader to justify his thinking with information from the text.

For Further Reading

Tierney, R. J., & Readence, J. E. (2005). *Reading strategies and practices: A compendium* (6th ed.). Boston: Allyn & Bacon.

Tompkins, G. E. (2004). *Fifty literacy strategies: Step by step* (2nd ed.). Upper Saddle River, NJ: Merrill/Prentice Hall.

■ Echo Reading   *Targeted Reading Levels 1–4*

Description Echo reading is a form of modeling oral reading in which the teacher reads a line of a story and the student echoes her model by reading the same line, imitating her intonation and phrasing.

Text Any text that is well written

Predominant Focus of Instruction

1. Processing focus: print
2. Instructional phase: during reading
3. Response mode emphasized: oral
4. Strategy emphasized: prediction
5. Skill emphasized: fluency
6. Source of information: reader-based
7. Type of instruction: implicit

Procedure

1. The teacher selects a text approximately 200 words long that is near frustration level reading for the student.
2. The teacher reads the first line of the text, accentuating appropriate phrasing and intonation.
3. Immediately, the student reads the same line, modeling the teacher's example.
4. The teacher and the student read in echo fashion for the entire passage, increasing the amount of text when the student can imitate the model.

Modifications

1. Echo reading is an effective intervention with repeated readings (see "Repeated Readings" in this part). After the first reading, the teacher and student can echo read those sentences that prompted a string of miscues or errors.
2. Echo reading can also be used in conjunction with chunking (see "Chunking" in this part) so the student can hear the way the teacher chunks language into thoughts.

Further Applications

Basic View of Reading Reading is a reader-based process in which a student matches what he hears with the text. The reader must read fluently to integrate the meaning with the text on the page.

Patterns of Strengths and Strategies Echo reading is most appropriate for the student who needs the teacher to model fluent oral reading and needs to repeat that model immediately in order to remember how the text sounded.

Learner Patterns That Produce Increased Engagement

1. For an extremely slow reader who needs to hear language read fluently, the teacher reads each sentence in thought units so this reader can read fluently with intonation.

*2. For a passive reader who has become word-bound and lost the flow of language, this technique allows him to hear fluent oral reading and immediately imitate the model.

*3. For a learner who has become extremely word-bound by an overemphasis on decoding, echo reading shows him how to use sentence meaning as well as the model to increase oral reading fluency.

*4. For a learner who refuses to follow the teacher when using the impress method, echo reading provides a clear model for this student to follow.

For Further Reading

Cunningham, P. M., & Allington, R. L. (2003). *Classrooms that work: They can all read and write* (3rd ed.). New York: Longman.

Tierney, R. J., & Readence, J. E. (2005). *Reading strategies and practices: A compendium* (6th ed.). Boston: Allyn & Bacon.

■ Experience-Text-Relationship   Targeted Reading Levels: All levels

Description   Experience-text-relationship (ETR) is specifically designed to use children's experiences to teach new concepts and new words in the story. In this technique, the teacher spends time showing students the relationships between what they know and what they are reading, both before and after reading the story. It is specifically designed for use with multicultural students (Au, 1993).

Text   Stories with an interesting theme or plot that can sustain an in-depth discussion

Predominant Focus of Instruction

1. Processing focus: meaning
2. Instructional phase: before and after reading
3. Response mode emphasized: oral discussion
4. Strategy emphasized: elaboration
5. Skill emphasized: nonliteral and literal comprehension
6. Source of information: reader-based phasing to text-based
7. Type of instruction: implicit

Procedure

1. The teacher chooses an appropriate text.
2. The teacher reads the selected passage to decide the theme, topic, and important points.
3. The teacher thinks about what students know related to the theme, topic, and important points.
4. The teacher formulates general questions that will initiate a discussion about what students know.
5. The teacher begins the instruction with a general discussion of what students know. (This step is the *experience phase* of the lesson and is student-initiated.)
6. The teacher uses the information generated to tie students' experiences directly to the story. She uses pictures and information that come directly from the story. (This step is teacher-directed.)
7. She asks students to make a prediction based on the discussion (student input).
8. Then, if necessary, the teacher sets other purposes for reading (teacher input).
9. The students read a portion of the story to see whether their predictions are right. This activity begins the *text phase* of the lesson.
10. The teacher returns to predictions and asks students what they have learned so far about these predictions.
11. The teacher sets additional purposes.
12. The teacher calls attention to important information in the text if necessary.
13. The teacher alternates periods of silent reading and discussion until the entire story has been read.

14. When the entire story has been read, the teacher directs a discussion of the key ideas in the story.
15. She then compares the key ideas in the text to the key experiences of the students by returning to the information gained during the experience phase of the lesson. This process is called the *relationship phase* and is teacher-directed.
16. The teacher then contrasts the key ideas in the text with students' experiences.
17. The teacher summarizes the main relationships after the discussion is complete.
18. Finally, the teacher recommends that students use the ETR steps when they read on their own.

Further Applications

Basic View of Reading   Reading is an interactive process in which learners use what they know to interpret what the text says. Readers need assistance learning how to figure out what they know that is useful to interpret the text. They need assistance in making connections between this information and what the text says.

Patterns of Strengths and Strategies   The ETR technique is appropriate for students who need assistance in bringing their background knowledge to the text. It is especially useful for multicultural students who experience a gap between the way they talk about their experiences and the way an author describes those same experiences. This technique helps these students relate their own language and experiences to the text.

Learner Patterns That Produce Increased Engagement

*1. For a passive learner who reads text without relating what he knows, ETR focuses on the student's experience during every step of the lesson.
*2. For a passive learner who will not venture a guess while reading, ETR gives him the tools to make a guess.

For Further Reading

Au, K. (1993). *Literacy instruction in multicultural settings.* New York: Harcourt Brace Jovanovich.

Taylor, B., Harris, L., Pearson, P. D., & Garcia, G. (1995). *Reading difficulties: Instruction and assessment.* New York: McGraw-Hill.

Feature Analysis Grid   *Targeted Reading Levels: All levels*

Description   A feature analysis grid is a technique to develop word meanings by graphing the major characteristics of target words. Key words are compared as to how they are alike and how they are different.

Text   Isolated words that are associated in categories

Predominant Focus of Instruction

1. Processing focus: meaning
2. Instructional phase: before and after reading
3. Response mode emphasized: oral discussion
4. Strategy emphasized: elaboration
5. Skill emphasized: word meaning
6. Source of information: reader-based
7. Type of instruction: explicit

Procedure

1. The teacher selects categories and words to analyze.
2. The teacher makes a feature analysis grid with a column of words to analyze.

CATEGORY: LANDSCAPES

New and Known Words	Important Characteristics				
	Trees	Water	Rocks	Snow	Sand
Mountains	+	+	+	+	−
Deserts	−	+	−	?	+

3. The teacher and students discuss the characteristics of the first word.
4. The teacher adds the characteristics across the top of the grid, indicating the important characteristics with a plus in the respective squares of the grid.
5. The teacher and students then discuss the second target word.
6. The teacher and students evaluate this word according to the important features on the grid. The teacher puts a plus on those characteristics that the second target word has and a minus on those that it does not have.
7. The teacher adds any new important characteristics, indicating those with a plus in the appropriate square on the grid. The teacher and students discuss any uncertain responses. In the example, deserts consist mainly of sand, but there are some snow deserts.

8. The teacher and students discuss how the two words are alike and how they are different.
9. The procedure is repeated for other words. The teacher adds important characteristics as needed.
10. The teacher adds other words that are prevalent in the students' oral vocabularies to make comparisons between what is new and what is already known.

Further Applications

Basic View of Reading   Reading is an interactive process based on what the reader already knows about the words used in the text. Comprehension is facilitated by understanding the specific attributes of the words used in a passage.

Patterns of Strengths and Strategies   The feature analysis grid is most appropriate for students who have a well-developed background of experiences but who overgeneralize word meanings, failing to see the likenesses and differences between specific definitional meanings. For these students, the graphic representation of important characteristics organizes the prior knowledge into specific linguistic categories.

Learner Patterns That Produce Increased Engagement

1. For a learner who has difficulty drawing comparisons among word meanings but has verbal fluency and analyzes individual words by their major features, this techniques allows him to compare and contrast the major features of words at the same time.
2. For a divergent thinker who notices features other than the major characteristics but easily understands the grid and the relationships among word meanings, this technique focuses his attention on the key features of the words.
*3. For a passive learner who does not think about the differences among words, this technique helps him think and talk about how words are alike and different.

For Further Reading

Gunning, T. G. (1998). *Assessing and correcting reading and writing difficulties*. Boston: Allyn & Bacon.

Johns, J. L., & Lenski, S. (2001). *Improving reading: A handbook of strategies* (3rd ed.). Dubuque, IA: Kendall/Hunt.

Framed Rhyming Innovations *Targeted Reading Levels K–3*

Description   The framed innovations approach is the rewriting of a predictable book that has rhymes using a structured frame. The teacher and student rewrite the predictable book using the frame but changing key words.

Text   Predictable books

Predominant Focus of Instruction

1. Processing focus: print
2. Instructional phase: after reading
3. Response mode emphasized: writing
4. Strategy emphasized: prediction
5. Skill emphasized: word identification and word analysis
6. Source of information: reader-based and text-based
7. Type of instruction: explicit

Procedure

1. The teacher selects a familiar predictable book that can be easily rewritten and has rhyme. For instance, *I Was Walking Down the Road* by Sarah Barchas can easily be rewritten and has rhyming phrases.
2. The teacher prepares a frame for rewriting the predictable book. For *I Was Walking Down the Road,* she would write

Complete frame

I was walking down the road.

Then I saw a little toad.

I caught it.

I picked it up.

I put it in the cage.

Frame for innovation

I was _____.

Then I saw _____.

I caught it.

I picked it up.

I put it in the cage.

3. The teacher and the student read the predictable book.
4. The teacher presents the frame for the innovation.

5. The teacher and student reread the complete frame first.
6. The teacher prompts the student for each blank in the frame. She might say, "What are you going to pick up?" The student suggests a frog and writes the word in the blank. "Then I saw a little frog."
7. After the student decides what is going to be picked up, then he generates a rhyming word to go with it that makes sense in the first sentence.

frog

dog

log

8. The student rewrites the first line. In this case he thinks of something that fits with "I saw a little frog." The student said, "I was running with my dog." He writes this line below the frame and rewrites the rest of the phrase.
9. This procedure is repeated several times so that the student can make his own book.
10. The student and teacher make a book based on the rewriting of the framed predictable book.

Further Applications

Basic View of Reading   Reading is an interactive process. By using story patterns that rhyme, students have to use their own knowledge about rhymes in words and synthesize sounds to make that rhyme. But they also have to make sure the word fits with the story pattern. This approach will facilitate word analysis and sentence comprehension.

Patterns of Strengths and Strategies   The framed rhyming innovations approach is most appropriate for students who have facility with language and phonemic awareness. If the student uses his own language and sense of phonic analogies, then this approach matches his own way for figuring out words.

Learner Patterns That Produce Increased Engagement

*1. For a learner who readily thinks of the rhymes in words and sees the analogous relationship among words, this approach uses the strength of seeing patterns to develop print processing.
*2. For an extremely creative verbal student who easily thinks of words that will fit the story, this approach increases the knowledge of word patterns and phonic analogies.

For Further Reading

Morrow, L., & Walker, B. (1997). *The reading team: A handbook for volunteer tutors K–3.* Newark, DE: International Reading Association.

Generative-Reciprocal Inference Procedure   *Targeted Reading Levels 2–8*

Description   The generative-reciprocal inference procedure (GRIP) is an instructional procedure for teaching children how to make inferences in both reading and writing. It involves reading and writing short paragraphs that require making an inference. After the teacher models the inferencing procedure, students, in pairs, write and exchange paragraphs that require an inference.

Text   Constructed by students and teacher

Predominant Focus of Instruction

1. Processing focus: meaning
2. Instructional phase: during reading
3. Response mode emphasized: written
4. Strategy emphasized: prediction and monitoring
5. Skill emphasized: nonliteral comprehension
6. Source of information: reader-based
7. Type of instruction: explicit

Procedure

1. The teacher selects a short paragraph to model how to make an inference.
2. The teacher puts the paragraph on the board or an overhead projector and highlights key words as the paragraph is read aloud. For example,

   Dennis looked surprised. *He had not intended it to happen. It was just that getting the* dog food *was difficult because it was* behind the table. *"It was my new* lamp,*" said Mrs. Wilson. "I just purchased it yesterday."*

   What had Dennis done?
3. The teacher explains that an inference is figuring out the key idea that is not in the text by using the key words in the text.
4. The teacher justifies how she figured out the inference by explaining how she used the text clues together with what she knew.
5. The teacher uses several more example paragraphs, letting the students make and justify the inference until they understand the procedure. The suggested sequence is the following:
   a. The teacher marks key words, the students make the inference, and the teacher explains the justification.
   b. The students mark the key words; the teacher makes the inference and explains the reasons.
   c. The students mark the key words and make the inference; the teacher explains the reasons.
   d. The students mark the key words, make the inference, and explain their reasoning.

6. Students write their own inference paragraphs in pairs, starting by creating a list of five or more key words.
7. Students write the paragraph without telling the inference.
8. In groups of four (two pairs), students exchange paragraphs.
9. Students mark key words, make an inference, and explain their thinking to one another.
10. Students discuss their thinking, giving each other feedback about the inferencing process.

Further Applications

Basic View of Reading   Reading is a socially constructed process in which learners use what they know to interpret what is written in the text. Readers need assistance learning how to identify key words in the text that can be used to predict unstated information and meaning. They also need assistance justifying how the text information and what they know support the inference.

Patterns of Strengths and Strategies   The GRIP technique is appropriate for students who need assistance in identifying key words that can be used in making inferences by using these words and what they already know.

Learner Patterns That Produce Increased Engagement

*1. For a passive learner who reads text without figuring out the unstated ideas needed to interpret text, GRIP helps focus how information in the text can suggest ideas not directly stated in the text.
*2. For a passive learner who does not identify important textual information to make inferences, GRIP shows him how selecting key information can facilitate thinking.

For Further Reading

Reutzel, D. R., & Cooter, R. B. (2004). *Teaching children to read: From basals to books* (4th ed.). Upper Saddle River, NJ: Merrill/Prentice Hall.

■ *Graphic Organizers*   *Targeted Reading Levels 3–12*

Description   The graphic organizer technique is designed to provide a visual representation of the main concepts in content-area readings. By conceptually arranging the key words in a chapter, the teacher and students develop an idea framework for relating unfamiliar vocabulary words and concepts.

Text   Expository text

Predominant Focus of Instruction

1. Processing focus: meaning
2. Instructional phase: before reading
3. Response mode emphasized: oral discussion with graphic information
4. Strategy emphasized: elaboration
5. Skill emphasized: word meaning and literal comprehension
6. Source of information: text-based
7. Type of instruction: explicit

Procedure

1. The teacher chooses a chapter from a textbook.
2. The teacher selects key vocabulary words and concepts.
3. The teacher arranges the key words into a diagram that shows how the key words interrelate.
4. The teacher adds a few familiar words to the diagram so students can connect their prior knowledge with the new information.
5. The teacher presents the graphic organizer on the chalkboard or an overhead transparency. As she presents the organizer, she explains the relationships.
6. Students are encouraged to explain how they think the information is related.
7. Students read the chapter, referring as needed to the graphic organizer.
8. After reading the selection, students may return to the graphic organizer to clarify and elaborate concepts.

Modifications

1. Students can generate their own graphic organizers after they read the chapter. In this situation, graphic organizers are an implicit instructional technique.
2. Students can work in cooperative learning groups to construct a graphic organizer after they read. This adds a socio-interactive aspect to the technique.

Further Applications

Basic View of Reading Reading is an active process in which learners use what they know to elaborate and extend what the text says. By constructing a visual map of word relationships, the teacher helps create an idea framework prior to reading the information.

Patterns of Strengths and Strategies The graphic organizer technique is appropriate for students who profit from a visual framework relating unfamiliar words and ideas to known information. It is especially useful for highly visual students who profit from seeing relationships in order to tie them to what they are reading.

Learner Patterns That Produce Increased Engagement

1. For a reader who thinks in visual images by relating patterns of information, graphic organizers help relate and elaborate topic knowledge.
*2. For a reader who reads without relating what he knows to the text, graphic organizers help him relate what he knows to unfamiliar concepts.
*3. For the passive reader who reads words without defining their meaning or conceptualizing how words relate, graphic organizers help him focus on new word meanings and concepts.

For Further Reading

Gipe, J. P. (2002). *Multiple paths to literacy: Classroom techniques for struggling readers* (5th ed.). Upper Saddle River, NJ: Merrill/Prentice Hall.

Tierney, R. J., & Readence, J. E. (2005). *Reading strategies and practices: A compendium* (6th ed.). Boston: Allyn & Bacon.

Guided Reading   Targeted Reading Levels 1–6

Description   Guided reading is used to develop reading abilities by having children read "just right" trade books that provide a slight challenge as the teacher provides a model for how to read the particular book. With the teacher model and guidance, the student assumes more independent reading behaviors.

Text   Leveled trade books

Predominant Focus of Instruction

1. Processing focus: print and meaning
2. Instructional phase: before, during, and after reading
3. Response mode emphasized: discussion
4. Strategy emphasized: prediction and monitoring
5. Skill emphasized: word recognition and literal comprehension
6. Source of information: text-based and reader-based
7. Type of instruction: implicit

Procedure

1. The teacher assesses the children's reading performance using leveled books. Their instructional level is reached when they have 90% accuracy in word recognition.
2. Students are placed into guided reading groups based on their instructional level. As the year progresses, children are regrouped based on reading level.
3. For younger children, the teacher pages through the book discussing the pictures.
4. The teacher guides the learning by reading the book aloud and discussing the book with the children.
5. Children are supported as they read along with the teacher. Young children are encouraged to use their finger to point to the words as they read.
6. Children are focused on print concepts and reading the text using multiple reading strategies. These strategies involve predicting, sampling, confirming, cross-checking, and self-correcting using the cueing system.
7. Children reread the text while the teacher listens to the children reading orally. The teacher prompts children to use cues to figure out words.
8. Children engage in retelling the story to each other while the teacher guides them to focus on what happened in the beginning, middle, and end.
9. Children engage in projects that extend their story understanding.
10. Children take guided reading books home to read to family members.

Further Applications

Basic View of Reading   Reading is a socio-interactive process in which children read with the teacher to create meaning. Through sharing information in a small group, children refine their use of print strategies and their understanding.

Patterns of Strengths and Strategies   Guided reading is most appropriate for students who can learn to read in a small group and readily understand how to figure out words.

Learner Patterns That Produce Increased Engagement

1. For a reader who profits by following the teacher's model, guided reading helps this student integrate the cueing systems.
2. For a learner who profits from hearing the whole story read at once, guided reading instruction helps this student create an expectation for the printed words.
*3. For a reader who is bound by the text and believes that reading means getting the words right, guided reading helps the reader think about the overall meaning and use this understanding to self-correct mistakes.

For Further Reading

Fountas, I. C., & Pinnell, G. S. (1996). *Guided reading: Good first teaching for all children.* Portsmouth, NH: Heinemann.

Reutzel, D. R., & Cooter, Jr., R. B. (2003). *Strategies for reading assessment and instruction: Helping every child succeed* (2nd ed.). Upper Saddle River, NJ: Merrill/Prentice Hall.

◼ *Herringbone Technique* *Targeted Reading Levels 5–12*

Description The herringbone technique develops comprehension of the main idea by plotting the *who, what, when, where, how,* and *why* questions on a visual diagram of a fish skeleton. Using the answers to the *wh* questions, the student writes the main idea across the backbone of the fish diagram.

Text Particularly suited for expository text; can be used for narrative text

Predominant Focus of Instruction

1. Processing focus: meaning
2. Instructional phase: during and after reading
3. Response mode emphasized: written response and oral discussion
4. Strategy emphasized: elaboration
5. Skill emphasized: literal comprehension
6. Source of information: text-based
7. Type of instruction: implicit with some explicit

Procedure

1. The teacher selects a text at the appropriate reading level.
2. The teacher constructs a visual diagram of the herringbone.
3. The teacher tells the student to record the answers to the questions on the diagram (see accompanying figure).
   a. Who is the author talking about?
   b. What did they do?
   c. When did they do it?

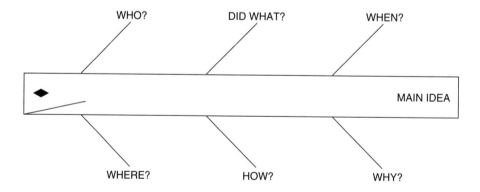

   d. Where did they do it?
   e. How did they do it?
   f. Why did they do it?

4. The student reads to find the answers and records the answers on the diagram.
5. After the information is recorded, the teacher shows the student how each answer fits into a slot in a main idea sentence.
6. The student writes a main idea, using the information from the herringbone diagram.
7. The teacher duplicates sheets with the herringbone diagram, and students complete the diagram on their own.
8. The diagram becomes a tool for discussion of readings. During the discussion, the teacher and students compare their answers and their rationales.

Further Applications

Basic View of Reading   Reading is a text-based process in which the reader uses the facts in the text to construct a main idea.

Patterns of Strengths and Strategies   The herringbone technique is most appropriate for students who need a visual structure to draw relationships between the facts in a text and the main idea. For these students, the technique records the information so that it can be organized into a whole.

Learner Patterns That Produce Increased Engagement

1. For a learner who has difficulty organizing factual information to form a main idea, this technique shows him how the facts support the main idea.
*2. For a learner who has problems identifying the important facts that are used to form a main idea, this technique helps him identify important information.
*3. For a learner who has difficulty identifying the factual information that he used to construct a main idea, this technique can be modified so that first the student writes the main idea and then rereads the text to find the facts that support the main idea.

For Further Reading

Gipe, J. P. (2002). *Multiple paths to literacy: Classroom techniques for struggling readers* (5th ed.). Upper Saddle River, NJ: Merrill/Prentice Hall.

Johns, J. L., & Lenski, S. (2001). *Improving reading: Strategies and resources* (3rd ed.). Dubuque, IA: Kendall/Hunt.

Imagery Instruction

Description   Imagery instruction uses sensory images related to the story line to increase active comprehension and activate background knowledge about (a) situations and characters in a story or (b) key concepts in expository text.

Text   Narrative text or concepts in expository text

Predominant Focus of Instruction

1. Processing focus: meaning
2. Instructional phase: before reading
3. Response mode emphasized: oral discussion
4. Strategy emphasized: prediction and monitoring
5. Skill emphasized: nonliteral comprehension
6. Source of information: reader-based
7. Type of instruction: implicit (can be adapted to explicit)

Procedure

1. The teacher selects a text.
2. The teacher identifies key events and characters or key concepts, depending on the type of text.
3. The teacher writes a guided journey that uses these key items. In the journey, the teacher intersperses calming statements with the story events and character descriptions or the key concepts. The following is an example that might be used prior to reading:

   Close your eyes. . . . and relax in your chair. . . . Now listen to the noises in the room. . . . Can you hear them? Feel the temperature of the room. . . . Now turn the noises of this room into the sounds of a meadow. . . . What kind of day is it? You can hear a river. . . . Begin walking toward the river. . . . You are closer. . . . closer. . . . closer to the river. . . . As you reach the river. . . . you see a boat. . . . Walk toward the boat. . . . You get in the boat and begin to float. . . . down. . . . down. . . . down the river you float. . . . The current or waves begin to rush faster. . . . faster. . . . faster. . . . You see rocks and boulders ahead. . . . You are steering the boat through the rapids. . . . I will leave you now. . . . When you have finished your journey. . . . you may return to this room. . . . and open your eyes.

4. For narrative text, the teacher uses the key events to develop the guided imagery, but she leaves the problem in the story unresolved. The students are to finish the story in their minds.
5. For expository text, the teacher develops a guided imagery that illustrates the attributes of the key concepts.
6. The teacher has the students relax in their chairs and think of sounds and smells relating to the setting. Then she reads the prompt or the journey in a calm, serene voice, interspersing action statements with calming statements.

7. The teacher tells the students to return to the classroom when they have completed their journeys in the mind.
8. The students can share their images with a partner.
9. Students read the selection to compare their journeys with the text.

Modification   The guided imagery can form the basis for a dictated language experience story. The teacher uses targeted sight words to compose the guided imagery (see "Language Experience Approach").

Further Applications

Basic View of Reading   Reading is an active process that uses personal images (reader-based inferencing) to create meaning. As the student reads, he forms an expectation for meaning that is represented by images of specific events. The student refines his model of meaning (basically images) when he reads.

Patterns of Strengths and Strategies   Imagery instruction is a technique for students who prefer to create images while they read. It is appropriate for the reflective thinker who refers to specific events and images when discussing text. Using guided imagery helps him translate images into a verbal response.

Learner Patterns That Produce Increased Engagement

1. For the thinker who uses images to construct meaning that often results in changing the story line to fit his model of meaning, this technique helps him see how his own ideas and images affect his comprehension.
2. For an imaginative thinker who enjoys sharing his images and comparing them to the text, this technique allows him to use this strength when reading.
3. For a reflective thinker who uses images instead of words when thinking, this technique allows images to be connected with words.
*4. For the passive reader who does not check what he knows while he reads, learning to image can increase his elaboration and monitoring of what he is reading.
*5. For the literal thinker who seldom constructs images, imagery instruction provides a support for him to construct images before reading, thus increasing his understanding.

For Further Reading
Gambrell, L. B., & Jawitz, P. B. (1993). Mental imagery, text illustrations, and children's story comprehension and recall. *Reading Research Quarterly, 28,* 264–276.

◼ Impress Method   *Targeted Reading Levels K–5*

Description   The impress method uses unison oral reading between the teacher and the student. The teacher and student sit side by side, with the teacher reading out loud slightly louder and ahead of the student, modeling fluent and expressive oral reading.

Text   Self-selected text is recommended.

Predominant Focus of Instruction

1. Processing focus: print
2. Instructional phase: during reading
3. Response mode emphasized: oral production
4. Strategy emphasized: prediction
5. Skill emphasized: fluency and word identification
6. Source of information: reader-based
7. Type of instruction: implicit

Procedure

1. The student and the teacher select a text that is near the student's frustration-level reading and about 200 words long.
2. The teacher and the student read the text in unison. The teacher reads slightly ahead of, and slightly louder than, the student.
3. The teacher sits on the right side of the student and reads with the student.
4. The teacher moves her finger along the line of print so that the student's eyes can follow the reading.
5. The student's eyes follow the line of print as he reads.
6. As the student gains success through understanding the context, the teacher gradually lets him take the lead.
7. At this time, the teacher releases her lead in reading; however, she supplies difficult words when needed.

Modifications

1. Unison choral reading can be used with a group of students.
2. The textual characteristics seem to influence the effectiveness of impress reading. Rhythmic and repetitive texts seem to increase the student's participation. A good source is Shel Silverstein's *Where the Sidewalk Ends.*

Further Applications

Basic View of Reading   Reading is a process of accurate word identification in which automatic word identification precedes understanding. Therefore, reading is a text-based process. An abundance of reading errors contributes to an incorrect visual form being imprinted in memory. Therefore, accurate word identification is increased by unison reading, with the teacher modeling fluent oral reading.

Patterns of Strengths and Strategies   The impress method is most appropriate for students who make a series of miscues without using passage meaning to self-correct the miscues, which is often the result of reading at frustration level for an extended period of time. In the impress method, the student follows the teacher's model and imitates her fluent, accurate oral reading.

Learner Patterns That Produce Increased Engagement

1. For a learner who relies heavily on background knowledge when reading orally and who does not attend to the graphic cues, the impress method establishes accurate identification of words through use of the overall textual meaning.
*2. For a nonfluent reader who is word-bound because of a heavy emphasis on phonic instruction, this method can rapidly increase oral reading fluency by providing a model of fluent reading.
*3. For a nonreader who has not established a sight vocabulary, this technique can develop the student's sight vocabulary, particularly when high-interest material is used.

For Further Reading

McCormick, S. (2003). *Instructing students who have literacy problems.* Upper Saddle River, NJ: Merrill/Prentice Hall.

Rasinski, T., & Padak, N. (2004). *Effective reading strategies: Teaching children who find reading difficult* (3rd ed.). Upper Saddle River, NJ: Merrill/Prentice Hall.

■ *Journal Writing* *Targeted Reading Levels: All levels*

Description   Journal writing is a written response from students of their understanding and exploration of ideas related to reading or a particular unit of study.
In notebooks, students write about their reactions to new information, ask questions, elaborate new understandings, and so on. The teacher responds to these
ideas.

Text   Self-generated written responses

Predominant Focus of Instruction

1. Processing focus: meaning
2. Instructional phase: after reading
3. Response mode emphasized: written discourse
4. Strategy emphasized: elaboration
5. Skill emphasized: nonliteral comprehension
6. Source of information: reader-based
7. Type of instruction: implicit
8. Type of cognitive processing: simultaneous

Procedure

1. The teacher secures writing notebooks. She can use bound composition notebooks, student-made books of stapled pages, or loose-leaf notebooks.
2. The teacher explains that a journal is a written explanation of the student's
   thinking about a topic. It is like writing a letter to the teacher about the topic.
3. She tells the students she will comment personally on what is written.
4. The teacher shows the students an example from a journal. (The teacher first
   secures permission from the writer.)
5. She tells the students that they are to write about the focus topic.
6. The teacher reads what the students write.
7. The teacher responds with questions or comments that encourage elaboration
   of the topic.
8. The students read the teacher's comments.
9. The students write a response or elaborate new information.
10. The writing cycle continues.

Modifications   Many modifications can be made in the focus of journal writing.
Some common ones are described in the following list:

1. Dialogue journals are a personal communication between the teacher and the
   student. It has no designated topic, but rather is a personal exchange, like
   writing a letter to a friend. With it, students write important things about their
   life to their teacher. Although this kind of dialogue journal is more effective
   for some students than others, it is recommended as part of the diagnostic
   teaching session because it releases the structured format of directed and
   guided instruction.

2. Learning logs are specific journals about a unit of study. The teacher comments are to focus the students on aspects of their study, such as selecting and narrowing a topic, gathering information, organizing the information, elaborating and integrating concepts as well as evaluating the information learned.
3. In double-entry journals, notebook pages are divided in half. On the left-hand page, the student makes notes, diagrams, clusters, and observations while on the right-hand page, the student integrates this information into a coherent understanding.

Further Applications

Basic View of Reading   Reading is an active, reader-based process in which readers' personal understanding focuses thinking. Both reading and writing are constructive processes that are influenced by the desire to communicate ideas.

Patterns of Strengths and Strategies   Journal writing is most appropriate for simultaneous, high imagery students who enjoy communicating ideas through writing rather than talking. In this technique, ideas and understandings are communicated without an oral explanation or eye contact.

Learner Patterns That Produce Increased Engagement

1. For a learner who needs time to express his ideas in words, writing allows him to think through ideas without noticeably lengthy pauses.
2. For a visually orientated reader who prefers to communicate his ideas through writing rather than talking, journal writing allows him to put his thoughts into words without talking.
*3. For a passive reader who does not realize that reading and writing are constructive processes, this technique allows him to experience reading and writing as communicating learning.
*4. For a text-bound reader who does not use his personal understanding of the world to interpret information, journals show him how a writer uses personal understanding to compose text.

Using the Technique as a Diagnostic Lesson   For journal writing to be effective, a majority of the following statements must be answered in the affirmative:

Yes	No	
_____	_____	1. The student can write (produce letters) fairly easily.
_____	_____	2. The student likes to communicate his ideas in writing.
_____	_____	3. The student uses the teacher's model to correct his own writing errors.

For Further Reading

Ruddell, M. R. (2005). *Teaching content reading and writing* (4th ed.). Hoboken, NJ: Wiley Publishers.

Short, K. G., Harste, J. C., & Burke, C. (1996). *Creating classrooms for authors and inquirers*. Portsmouth, NH: Heinemann.

K-W-L

Description   K-W-L is a technique used to direct students' reading and learning of content-area text. Before the text is read, students write what they already know about the topic as well as questions they would like to explore. After the text is read, students write what they learned about the topic.

Text   Especially suited for expository text, but can be applied to all text

Predominant Focus of Instruction

1. Processing focus: meaning
2. Instructional phase: before and after reading
3. Response mode emphasized: written with some discussion
4. Strategy emphasized: prediction and elaboration
5. Skill emphasized: literal and nonliteral comprehension
6. Source of information: reader-based phasing to text-based
7. Type of instruction: implicit

Procedure

1. The teacher chooses an appropriate topic and text.
2. The teacher introduces the K-W-L worksheet (see the accompanying figure).
3. The students brainstorm ideas about the topic.
4. The teacher writes this information on a chart or chalkboard.
5. Students write what they know under the K ("What I Know") column.
6. Together, the teacher and students categorize the K column.
7. Students generate questions they would like answered about the topic and write them in the W ("What I Want to Learn") column.
8. Students silently read the text and add new questions to the W column.
9. After reading, the students complete the L ("What I Learned") column.
10. The students and teacher review the K-W-L sheet to tie together what students knew and the questions they had with what they learned.

Modifications

1. The K-W-L Plus technique extends the after-reading phase to include organizing the information through webbing and writing a summary.
2. The information known and learned can be combined to form a book.
3. The technique can be modified to include a column for students to discuss "How" they learned new information (KWHL).

Further Applications

Basic View of Reading   Reading is a socio-interactive process in which learners share what they know to elaborate and extend what the text says. Readers need experience relating what they know, the questions they have, and what they have learned from text in order to actively construct meaning.

What I Know	What I Want to Learn	What I Learned

K-W-L TECHNIQUE

Note. Adapted from "K-W-L: A Teaching Model That Develops Active Reading of Expository Text" by Donna Ogle, 1986, *The Reading Teacher*, 39, pp. 564–570. Copyright 1986 by International Reading Association. Adapted by permission.

Patterns of Strengths and Strategies   The K-W-L technique is appropriate for students who need to talk and write about the topic prior to reading. It is especially useful for students who need to see concretely what they know to tie it to what they are reading.

Learner Patterns That Produce Increased Engagement

1. For a self-directed reader who does not readily elaborate what he learns as he reads, K-W-L helps this student expand and elaborate topic knowledge.
*2. For a reader who reads without relating what he knows to the text, K-W-L helps tie together what he knows and the text.
*3. For a passive reader who needs to see what he has learned in relation to what he knows, the K-W-L helps him assess the understanding he has developed through reading.

For Further Reading

Johns, J. L., & Lenski, S. (2001). *Improving reading: A handbook of strategies* (3rd ed.). Dubuque, IA: Kendall/Hunt.

Tierney, R. J., & Readence, J. E. (2005). *Reading strategies and practices: A compendium* (6th ed.). Boston: Allyn & Bacon.

Language Experience Approach

Targeted Reading Levels K–3

Description   The language experience approach (LEA) is a technique used for beginning reading instruction in which the child dictates a story to the teacher. The story becomes the text for instruction, and a collection of the stories becomes the child's first reader.

Text   The child's own language

Predominant Focus of Instruction

1. Processing focus: print
2. Instructional phase: before and during reading
3. Response mode emphasized: oral discussion
4. Strategy emphasized: prediction and monitoring
5. Skill emphasized: word identification
6. Source of information: reader-based
7. Type of instruction: implicit

Procedure

1. The teacher engages students in dialogue about a particular topic. A stimulating, engaging, and concrete topic tends to elicit more language from the students.
2. The students dictate a story while the teacher serves as secretary for the class.
3. Using leading questions, the teacher quides the students to develop a story line by using questions such as these: "What happened next? Is this what you wanted to say? How can you make a story using this information?"
4. The students and the teacher read the story simultaneously to revise any statements or phrases that are unclear to the students. The story is to follow the students' natural language patterns.
5. Then the teacher and students read the story *repeatedly* because repetition of the entire story will encourage a predictive set for the story.
6. Students are asked to read the story independently.
7. Activities to reinforce word identification are constructed from the story.
8. Chunk cards are developed using the words in the story. These cards are made by dividing the entire story into meaningful phrases, which are written on cards.
9. Initially, these chunk cards are flashed in the order in which they appear in the story. Later, they are mixed up. This activity maintains the sense of the whole while the whole is being broken into parts.
10. Stories are collated into anthologies that create the initial reading material for the student.
11. As words are repeatedly read in context, the teacher checks them off a word list, but does not assess this knowledge in isolation.

Further Applications

Basic View of Reading   Reading is an active, reader-based process. By reading his own story, the student will infer the consistency of printed language patterns. Because the story is based on his own experience, he continually uses this experience to remember the words in the story.

Patterns of Strengths and Strategies   Language experience is most appropriate for students who have facility with language and are reader-based thinkers. If a student predicts from his own experiences rather than the words in the text, then language experience matches his strategies (using what he knows); therefore, this technique facilitates word learning by asking the student to identify words using his own experiences.

Learner Patterns That Produce Increased Engagement

1. For a reader who uses prior knowledge to construct meaning, often resulting in overpredicting or guessing without identifying words by how they are written, LEA uses the student's strength (using prior knowledge) to facilitate word identification.
2. For an extremely verbal, creative student whose verbalization interferes with the mundane task of looking at words, LEA uses the strength (verbalization) to facilitate word identification.
*3. For a student who is unwilling to take a guess unless he is certain the response will be correct, LEA provides a text that allows the student to make a safe guess, using both what is on the page and what he remembers was written.
*4. For a learner who has had an overemphasis on phonics, language experience can increase his fluency and the predictive set.

For Further Reading

Tierney, R. J., & Readence, J. E. (2005). *Reading strategies and practices: A compendium* (6th ed.). Boston: Allyn & Bacon.
Tompkins, G. E. (2004). *Fifty literacy strategies: Step by step* (2nd ed.). Upper Saddle River, NJ: Merrill/Prentice Hall.

Literature Circles

Description   Literature circles are used to develop personal responses to literature by having students share their interpretations in a discussion group. By talking about the literature, students integrate the author's ideas and concepts with their own.

Text   Authentic children's literature

Predominant Focus of Instruction

1. Processing focus: meaning
2. Instructional phase: after reading
3. Response mode emphasized: oral discussion
4. Strategy emphasized: elaboration
5. Skill emphasized: nonliteral comprehension
6. Source of information: reader-based phasing into text-based
7. Type of instruction: implicit

Procedure

1. The teacher introduces several books by giving short summaries or book talks.
2. The students choose a book to read over the next two days or week.
3. After the books are read, the students reading the same book gather into a literature circle.
4. The discussion is open-ended, with the teacher beginning with an invitation such as "Tell me about this book" or "What was your favorite part?"
5. At the end of the discussion time, the group decides what they will talk about the next day.
6. As students become familiar with this format, the teacher becomes less involved in the discussion and lets the students take the lead.
7. The teacher's role in discussion includes these activities:
   a. Listening closely and focusing on students' ideas
   b. Supporting thinking and reflection by saying "Let's think more about that"
   c. Keeping the discussion focused on a theme
   d. Pointing out literary elements (characters, setting, and so on) and strategies (using background knowledge) and encouraging students to discuss them
8. At the conclusion of the discussion, group members can present their interpretation to the class as a "book talk."

Modifications

1. To add a writing component, students can keep a literature log so they can more easily share their ideas.
2. For some groups, the teacher may continue in the literature circle as a group member.

Further Applications

Basic View of Reading   Reading is a socio-interactive process in which the social context affects individual interpretation of text. Through sharing ideas in a peer group, students define and elaborate their ideas.

Patterns of Strengths and Strategy   The literature circle technique is appropriate for students who can discuss their ideas freely in a group. The dialogue helps these students elaborate their understanding of literature and connect that understanding to their experiences.

Learner Patterns That Produce Increased Engagement

1. For a self-directed reader who profits from sharing his ideas in a group, literature circles help this student verify and create interpretations.
2. For a self-directed reader who likes to share personal feelings about text but needs time to reflect on ideas before discussing, literature circles help this student connect his personal feelings with the text.
*3. For a reader who is bound by the text and believes that reading means getting right answers, literature circles allow this student to verbalize ideas in a safe environment and see how his peers think about a story.

For Further Reading

Fountas, I. C., & Pinnell, G. S. (1996). *Guided reading: Good first teaching for all children.* Portsmouth, NH: Heinemann.

Short, K. G., Harste, J. C., & Burke, C. (1996). *Creating classrooms for authors and inquirers.* Portsmouth, NH: Heinemann.

Making Words

Description   Making words is used to help readers develop the ability to spell words and apply this knowledge when decoding. In this procedure, children learn to make a six- or seven-letter word as they make smaller words. This activity is used with regular writing activities to increase the children's decoding ability.

Text   Letter cards

Predominant Focus of Instruction

1. Processing focus: print
2. Instructional phase: skill instruction
3. Response mode emphasized: oral
4. Strategy emphasized: monitoring
5. Skill emphasized: word identification and word analysis
6. Source of information: text-based
7. Type of instruction: implicit

Procedure

1. Before beginning, the teacher decides on the final word in the lesson and makes a list of the shorter words that can be made from its letters. She picks 10–15 words that include: (a) words that can be sorted for the patterns, (b) words of different lengths to provide challenging and easy work, (c) a proper name so they can be reminded to use capital letters, and (d) words with familiar meanings. She writes all the words on cards and orders them from shortest to longest so the order emphasizes letter patterns.
2. The teacher places the larger letter cards in a pocket chart or along the chalk ledge and gives the student a set of letters.
3. The teacher and student review the letter cards.
4. She tells the student to take two letters and make the first word. She says the word and uses it in a sentence.
5. The teacher has the student make the other words, indicating the number of letters needed and cues the student as to whether to change one letter, change letters around, or use all the letters.
6. The teacher reviews all the words in the lesson, saying and spelling each word and putting it on an index card.
7. The words are then sorted (see "Word Sorts") for phonic patterns. For example, all the words beginning with the same letter would be one sort; rhyming words are another sort, and so on.

Further Applications

Basic View of Reading   Learning to read means understanding how letters work within a word. Readers need to use their knowledge of letter patterns to figure out new words; therefore, reading is an interactive process. By listening closely to a word pronounced, the student can match the letters to the sounds in the words.

Patterns of Strengths and Strategies   The making words approach is most appropriate for students who can segment words into their sounds and match those sounds to the letters in the word. This technique builds on their strength and allows them to develop a system for decoding by analogy to key words.

Learner Patterns That Produce Increased Engagement

1. For a thinker who readily uses what he knows and manipulates visual information, this technique promotes understanding the sound relationships in words.
*2. For a passive learner who is phonetically aware but needs help focusing on the letters in words, this technique uses his strength of sound knowledge to enhance the decoding process.
*3. For a learner who can match sounds to letters, this technique helps him develop a system for using what he knows to figure out words.

For Further Reading

Cunningham, P. M., & Cunningham, J. W. (1992). Making words: Enhancing the invented spelling-decoding connection. *The Reading Teacher, 46*, 106–107.

Snow, C. E., Burns, M. S., & Griffin, P. (1998). *Preventing reading difficulties in young children.* Washington, DC: National Academy Press.

Making and Writing Words

Description Making and writing words (MWW) is used to help readers think about and make words using letters and letter patterns. In this procedure children think about the sounds in easy and hard words that are either pronounced by the teacher or match hints provided by the teacher. In this way this procedure works on spelling, decoding, and vocabulary knowledge.

Text Making and writing words worksheet

Predominant Focus of Instruction

1. Processing focus: print
2. Instructional phase: skill instruction
3. Response mode emphasized: written
4. Strategy emphasized: predicting and monitoring
5. Skill emphasized: word analysis
6. Source of information: text-based
7. Type of instruction: implicit

Procedure

1. In planning the lesson, the teacher decides on the final word in the lesson and makes a list of the shorter words that can be made from its letters. She picks 10–15 words that include: (a) words that can be sorted for the patterns, (b) words of different lengths to provide challenging and easy work, and (c) words with familiar meanings. She makes a list of the consonants and vowels that will be used.
2. The teacher instructs the students to write the consonants and vowels in the appropriate place on the MWW sheets (see accompanying figure).
3. The teacher either pronounces or gives cues for two- and three-letter words. For example, the teacher might say, "In box number one write a three-letter word that means a fury animal." The students would write *cat.*
4. The teacher gives clues for the other boxes. For example, she might say, "In the next three boxes, write words that belong to the *at* family."
5. The teacher works with the class through the remaining words she had planned.
6. The final word is always the "challenge word." Students are challenged to use all the letters to write the final word in the final box.
7. The teacher then asks students to write *transfer words*, which are words that are difficult but use the knowledge gained in the initial boxes.
8. Finally, the students cut out each box to form individual word cards to be used in word sorts. (See "Word Sorts" in this part.) For example, the students may sort all words in the *at* family.

Making and Writing Words

Vowels	Consonants

1	6	11
2	7	12
3	8	13
4	9	14
5	10	15

T-1	T-2	T-3

Source: Rasinski, Timothy. (1999). Making and writing words. *Reading Online,* an electronic journal of the International Reading Association. Reprinted with permission. Available at http://www.readingonline.org/articles/art_index.asp?HREF=/articles/words/rasinski_index.html.

Further Applications

Basic View of Reading   Reading involves understanding how letters work within a word. Readers use their knowledge of letter patterns to figure out new words; therefore, reading is an interactive process. By listening to clues about words, the students can predict what the word will be and then figure out the letter and letter patterns to write the word.

Patterns of Strengths and Strategies   The making and writing words approach is most appropriate for students who can segment words into their sounds and match those sounds to the letters in the word. This technique allows them to develop a system for decoding and using key words.

Learner Patterns That Produce Increased Engagement

1. For a reader who readily uses letter pattern knowledge and writes easily, the technique promotes understanding the sound relationships in words.
*2. For a passive learner who is phonetically aware but needs help focusing on letters, the technique asks him to write the sounds in the words he knows.
*3. For a thinker who readily thinks about what he knows, the technique offers a visual way to think about sounds in words.

Modification   Rather than writing unrelated words, the activity can focus on letter patterns. The teacher selects a multisyllabic word and identifies its letter patterns and individual letters. The teacher then writes the letters and letter patterns in the boxes rather than vowels and consonants.

For Further Reading
Rasinski, T. (1999). Making and writing words. *Reading Online*, Retrieved September 1, 2002, from http://readingonline.org/articles/words/rasinski.html.
Rasinski, T. (2001). Making and writing words using letter patterns. *Reading Online*, Retrieved September, 1, 2002, from http://readingonline.org/articles/rasinski/MWW_LP.html.

Opinion-Proof Approach   *Targeted Reading Levels 4–12*

Description   The opinion-proof approach is a technique designed to engage students in higher-level thinking skills by asking them to write opinions and supporting evidence about a selection. This technique emphasizes evaluative thinking, verification, and persuasive argument.

Text   Any kind that supports various points of view

Predominant Focus of Instruction

1. Processing focus: meaning
2. Instructional phase: after reading
3. Response mode emphasized: written discourse to oral discussion
4. Strategy emphasized: monitoring and elaboration
5. Skill emphasized: nonliteral comprehension
6. Source of information: reader-based supported by text-based
7. Type of instruction: implicit

Procedure

1. Students read a selected text.
2. The teacher guides the silent reading using an appropriate technique.
3. After the text is read, the teacher provides the students with an "Opinion-Proof" guide either on the chalkboard or a handout.
4. She explains that on the left side of the page the students are to write opinions about characters or events.
5. The teacher further explains that on the right side of the page, the students are to write proof for their opinions. This proof is to be derived directly from the text.
6. When students have completed their Opinion-Proof guide, they are to write an essay using their opinions with the supporting evidence they collected.
7. The teacher and students develop specific criteria for evaluating the essay. Some examples are "Is the evidence found in the text?" and "Does this evidence support my opinion?"
8. The teacher divides the class into groups or pairs.
9. The students share their essays and revise unclear ideas.

Modification   If writing an essay is difficult, the teacher may provide "framed paragraphs" with leading lines that introduce the opinion followed by the support. For example, "In this story, I believe. . . . The reason I think this is. . . . "

Further Applications

Basic View of Reading   Reading is a socio-interactive process in which the reader predicts and interprets information, using his own ideas based on information in the text. This interactive process begins with the reader using his own knowledge and then finding support in the text. Finally, the reader's understanding is shared and revised with classmates.

Patterns of Strengths and Strategies   The opinion-proof approach is most appropriate for students who need time to write and think about their ideas prior to discussion. The writing helps them elaborate their ideas, integrating both the text and background knowledge.

Learner Patterns That Produce Increased Engagement

1. For readers who use reader-based inferencing and are quiet and reflective, the opinion-proof allows them to have time to think through their ideas before discussion.
*2. For readers who are highly verbal and can write with ease but who are text-based, this approach uses their writing strength to lead them to tie the text to reader-based inferencing.
*3. For readers who use reader-based inferencing when comprehending text, the opinion-proof approach helps them return to the text to support, revise, and modify their thinking based on textual information.

For Further Reading

Manzo, A., & Manzo, U. (1990). *Content area reading: A heuristic approach.* Upper Saddle River, NJ: Merrill/Prentice Hall.

Paired Reading   *Targeted Reading Levels K–5*

Description   The paired reading technique uses joint reading aloud between two individuals. They sit together and read a story aloud simultaneously. One individual (another adult or child) serves as a model of fluent reading.

Text   Stories and poems

Predominant Focus of Instruction

1. Processing focus: print
2. Instructional phase: during reading
3. Response mode emphasized: oral reading
4. Strategy emphasized: prediction
5. Skill emphasized: fluency
6. Source of information: reader-based
7. Type of instruction: implicit

Procedure

1. The student and the teacher select a text that is interesting and not too long. The paired reading needs to be short.
2. Before beginning, the teacher and the student decide on a sign for the student to give when he is ready to read on his own and one for when he needs help.
3. The teacher and the student read the text in unison.
4. The teacher sets a pace that is appropriate for the text, modeling intonation and phrasing.
5. The teacher can move her finger along the line of print if necessary.
6. As the student gains success, he signals the teacher to stop reading aloud.
7. The student continues on his own.

Modifications

1. This technique is effective with peer tutoring when the teacher can divide the class into two groups and establish pairs for reading. Some teachers call this approach *partner reading*.
2. The pairs or partners can rate each other's fluency using a modified fluency scale (see Chapter 4 for fluency scale).

Further Applications

Basic View of Reading   Reading is a socio-interactive process in which fluency is developed as students read along with others. Using a model of a more fluent reader, the student readily integrates word recognition and comprehension as he reads.

Patterns of Strengths and Strategies   Paired reading is most appropriate for students who read slowly but accurately. The paired reading provides a model of fluent reading and increases the student's reading rate at the same time.

Learner Patterns That Produce Increased Engagement

1. For a learner who relies heavily on background knowledge when reading orally, paired reading allows him to attend to letters and meaning simultaneously.
2. For a highly social student who likes to interact with others and follow their model, this technique lets him use his preferences while practicing reading.
*3. For a nonfluent reader who is word-bound because of a heavy emphasis on phonic instruction, this method can increase reading fluency.

For Further Reading

Rasinski, T., & Padak, N. (2001). *From phonics to fluency: Effective teaching of decoding and reading fluency in the elementary school.* Upper Saddle River, NJ: Merrill/Prentice Hall.

Topping, K. (1989). Peer tutoring and paired reading: Combining two powerful techniques. *The Reading Teacher, 42,* 488–494.

Phonogram Approach   *Targeted Reading Levels 1–3*

Description   The phonogram approach is a structured program to introduce phonic principles by use of sound clusters within words. As whole words are introduced, the student is directed to look at the sound clusters in the words. Then the student finds similar letter clusters in new words and associates them with the known cluster words.

Text   Isolated words that have the same word patterns and text that contains these patterns

Predominant Focus of Instruction

1. Processing focus: print
2. Instructional phase: after reading
3. Response mode emphasized: oral discussion
4. Strategy emphasized: elaboration
5. Skill emphasized: word analysis
6. Source of information: text-based
7. Type of instruction: explicit

Procedure

1. The teacher presents isolated words that contain the letter cluster. For the *an* sound cluster, these words could be presented:

fan	can	candy
man	pan	fancy
ran	Stan	candle

2. The teacher pronounces the whole word and identifies letter names and letter sounds of that target cluster. For example:

   "In the word *fan,* the letter *f* goes *'f-f-f'* and the letters *a-n* go *'an'.*"

3. The teacher pronounces the letter sound or cluster sounds and asks the student for its name. For example:

   "In the word *fan,* what letter goes *'f-f-f'*?"

   "In the word *fan,* what letters go *'an'*?"

4. The teacher pronounces the letter name or cluster and asks the student for its sound. For example:

   "In the word *fan,* what sound does the *f* make?"

   "In the word *fan,* what sounds do *a-n* make?"

5. The teacher asks the student, "What is the word?"
6. Steps 2, 3, 4, and 5 are continued until the pattern is learned.

7. The teacher presents the words in sentences, and the student reads the sentences. For example:

The man canned the fancy candy.

Stan ran to fan the candle.

8. If a word cannot be decoded, the teacher directs the student to the letter cluster and asks for its name and sound. For example:

"Look at the word. Where is the *a-n*? What sounds do they make?

What's the first letter? What sound does it make?"

9. The teacher returns to the list of words and asks the student, "How are *can, candy,* and *canopy* alike, and how are they different?"

Further Applications

Basic View of Reading   Reading is a text-based process in which the student must learn to decode printed words before he can read for meaning. As such, the learner is explicitly taught the analogous sound relationships to enhance decoding.

Patterns of Strengths and Strategies   Looking for sound clusters in whole words is most appropriate for a visual learner. For this student, the approach facilitates word identification by using the visual patterns in already known words.

Learner Patterns That Produce Increased Engagement

*1. For a learner who needs direct instruction in forming phonic analogies among the words he already knows and new words he encounters, this technique uses his strength in identifying patterns.

*2. For an older student who needs a decoding strategy, this technique helps him use what he knows about context and word identification.

For Further Reading

Cunningham, P. M., & Allington, R. L. (2003). *Classrooms that work: They can all read and write* (3rd ed.). New York: Longman.

McCormick, S. (2003). *Instructing students who have literacy problems* (4th ed.). Upper Saddle River, NJ: Merrill/Prentice Hall.

■ *Prediction Logs*   *Targeted Reading Levels 4–12*

Description   Prediction logs are written accounts of students' active reading. At designated points, the students write a prediction and a reason for their prediction. As they read and write, they evaluate new information in relation to their previous predictions. The written record of their previous thoughts allows the students to analyze how they construct meaning.

Text   Narrative text

Predominant Focus of Instruction

1. Processing focus: meaning
2. Instructional phase: during reading
3. Response mode emphasized: written discourse
4. Strategy emphasized: prediction and monitoring
5. Skill emphasized: nonliteral comprehension
6. Source of information: reader-based
7. Type of instruction: implicit

Procedure

1. The teacher selects interesting stories so that readers can make predictions.
2. She decides on key turning points in the story and marks them for students.
3. The teacher prepares sheets with the following information:

Name of story:
Author:

	Prediction	Reason for Prediction
Section #1:		
Section #2:		

---

4. After the story is read, the prediction logs are used as a basis for discussing the story.
5. The students discuss how their interpretation developed through the story.
6. The students discuss the influence of personal understanding on comprehension.
7. The students write a reaction to the discussion, telling how their comprehension developed.

Further Applications

Basic View of Reading   Reading is a socio-interactive process in which the reader builds a model of meaning based on textual and nontextual information and then revises this model during a discussion. As a result of predicting and revising and the subsequent discussion, the reader builds his model of meaning; he predicts, monitors, and evaluates his interpretation in relation to the context of the situation.

Patterns of Strengths and Strategies   Prediction logs are most appropriate for the student who needs to evaluate how he forms his model of meaning. He often does not realize what information he uses from the text and what he already knows. Furthermore, he has difficulty thinking about how he forms his ideas and discussing them in a group. Prediction logs provide a method for analyzing how he constructs meaning before he participates in a group setting.

Learner Patterns That Produce Increased Engagement

1. For a learner who understands the story but does not understand how he constructs a response, prediction logs provide a record of his thoughts so that he can analyze them.
*2. For a passive learner who needs actively to engage in forming and revising his model of meaning, prediction logs have the student elaborate his understanding during the reading of the story.

For Further Reading

Macon, J. M., Bewell, D., & Vogt, M. (1991). *Responses to literature: Grades K–8*. Newark, DE: International Reading Association.

Short, K. G., Harste, J. C., & Burke, C. (1996). *Creating classrooms for authors and inquirers*. Portsmouth, NH: Heinemann.

Question-Answer Relationships

Targeted Reading Levels 4–8

Description The question-answer relationships (QAR) technique is used to identify the type of response necessary to answer a question. Knowledge about sources of information required to answer questions facilitates comprehension and increases a student's ability to participate in teacher-directed discussion.

Text Any text on which questions can be based

Predominant Focus of Instruction

1. Processing focus: meaning
2. Instructional phase: after reading
3. Response mode emphasized: oral discussion
4. Strategy emphasized: monitoring and elaboration
5. Skill emphasized: literal and nonliteral comprehension
6. Source of information: text-based with some reader-based
7. Type of instruction: explicit

Procedure

1. The teacher selects a text that can be the basis of different kinds of questions.
2. She introduces "right there" and "on my own" sources of information:
   a. "Right there" means that the answers are "right there" on the page, and the words from the text can be used to answer the question. The teacher points out that this source must often be used in answering a teacher's questions and in completing textbook exercises.
   b. "On my own" means that the students must fill in missing information, using what they know about what is in the text to answer the question. In this instance, the students must realize that they are "on their own" and use their own experience when they answer the question.
3. The teacher completes an example lesson identifying the kind of answer that is required by the question as well as giving the answer itself. She models the strategy of finding answers to questions and identifying the sources of information used.
4. The teacher introduces the "think and search" question-answer relationship. Here the student must read the text carefully and then "think and search" different parts of the text to find the answers that fit together to answer the question.
5. Then the teacher introduces "author and you" sources of information. In this response, the students need to think about what they know, what the author tells them, and how this information fits together.
6. The teacher completes an example lesson, identifying the kind of answer that is required by the questions as well as the answer. She models by using all four sources of information (*right there, think and search, author and you,* and *on my own*) and telling why and how the answers were obtained.

7. The students complete a third example lesson using a paragraph, the questions, and the answers. The students as a group identify the question-answer relationships. Students talk about reasons for a particular answer and the strategy used to obtain the answer.

8. The students complete a fourth example lesson using a paragraph, the questions, and the answers. Individually, students identify the question-answer relationship. Then students tell why they chose an answer, based on textual and nontextual information and the strategy used to obtain the answer.

Further Applications

Basic View of Reading   Reading is a socio-interactive process in which a reader's interpretation of text is based on textual and nontextual information. As they share their thinking, readers construct answers to questions, shifting between the text and what they know. Therefore, not only do students figure out answers to questions, but they also know the source of information they are using to construct the answer.

Patterns of Strengths and Strategies   QAR is most appropriate for students who rely heavily on one source of information to answer questions or who cannot answer questions. The technique requires these students to distinguish when it is appropriate to use their background knowledge and/or textual information to answer questions.

Learner Patterns That Produce Increased Engagement

*1. For a passive learner who is unaware of the various sources of information used to answer questions, this technique increases his active reading by asking him to evaluate how he got an answer.

*2. For a learner who relies heavily on background knowledge about the subject to answer questions, this technique shows him when and how he can use background knowledge effectively when he needs to use the text.

*3. For a text-bound learner who does not use what he already knows to answer questions, this technique shows him how to fill in missing information using what he knows.

For Further Reading

Reutzel, D. R., & Cooter, R. (2003). *Strategies for reading assessment and instruction: Helping every child succeed* (2nd ed.). Upper Saddle River, NJ: Merrill/Prentice Hall.

Question-Generation Strategy   *Targeted Reading Levels 4–12*

Description   Writing postreading questions uses student-generated questions to develop an understanding of the important information in the text. By deciding what to ask in their questions, students think about what is important in the text.

Text   Narrative or expository

Predominant Focus of Instruction

1. Processing focus: meaning
2. Instructional phase: after reading
3. Response mode emphasized: written
4. Strategy emphasized: elaboration
5. Skill emphasized: literal and nonliteral comprehension
6. Source of information: reader-based because the student writes the question, but can be text-based if the student uses only the text
7. Type of instruction: initially explicit, then rapidly moves to implicit

Procedure

1. The teacher selects a text at the appropriate level.
2. She discusses how to write questions:
   a. A question has an answer.
   b. A good question begins with a question word like *who, what, when, where,* or *why.*
   c. A good question can be answered using information in the story.
   d. A good question asks about important information in the story.
3. The teacher selects a short paragraph and models writing questions about the important information in the text.
4. The students write questions after they read a short paragraph.
5. The students answer their questions.
6. The students compare their questions and answers with the teacher's questions and answers.
7. The teacher gives feedback about the importance of the questions.
8. The students write questions about the important information in their assigned text.
9. The students answer their questions.
10. The students compare their questions and answers with the teacher's questions and answers.

Modifications

1. Instead of step 2, the teacher uses story grammar questions (e.g., "Who was the leading character?"). Then she has the students make story-specific questions (see "Story Mapping").

2. Instead of step 10, the teacher allows the students to share their questions and answers in small groups, which makes the technique more socio-interactive.
3. The teacher uses postgenerated questioning with book reports. After reading a book, the student writes his questions on cards. Then other students who have read the same book can use the cards to answer questions about the book.

Further Applications

Basic View of Reading   Reading is an interactive process in which the reader selects important textual information by constructing questions using his background knowledge and selected information.

Patterns of Strengths and Strategies   Postgenerated questioning is most appropriate for students who have facility with word identification and word meaning but have difficulty studying for tests. For these students, this approach requires them to read text in order to formulate questions about the important information in the text.

Learner Patterns That Produce Increased Engagement

1. For a learner who knows the meanings of words but depends on teacher questioning to interpret the important information, this technique helps the student become more independent by having him write the questions before comparing them with the teacher's questions.
2. For a learner who has not learned to ask himself questions to monitor what he needs to remember when he reads, this technique encourages him to monitor his understanding by asking himself questions.
*3. For a learner who tries to remember all the details rather than focusing on the important facts, by writing and comparing questions he thinks about what is important to remember.

For Further Reading

Barr, R., Blachowicz, C., Katz, C., & Kaufman, B. (2002). *Reading diagnosis for teachers: An instructional approach* (4th ed.). White Plains, NY: Longman.

Readers Theater   **Targeted Reading Levels 2–5**

Description   Readers theater is a dramatic interpretation of a play script through oral interpretive reading. The story theme and character development are conveyed through intonation, inflection, and fluency of oral reading.

Text   Scripts designed for the appropriate number of readers

Predominant Focus of Instruction

1. Processing focus: print and meaning
2. Instructional phase: after reading
3. Response mode emphasized: oral
4. Strategy emphasized: elaboration
5. Skill emphasized: nonliteral comprehension and fluency
6. Source of information: reader-based and text-based
7. Type of instruction: implicit

Procedure

1. The teacher selects a narrative text at the appropriate reading level and constructs a play script.
2. The teacher presents a brief description of the characters, setting, events, and problem.
3. The students select or are assigned appropriate parts to read.
4. The students preview the scripts silently.
5. Standing in a line in front of a seated audience, the students read the scripts orally.
6. No props or costumes are used.
7. The students convey the story line by their intonation and phrasing.
8. Listeners must use their imaginations to interpret the story line.

Modifications

1. A readers theater can be developed from the text that the students are reading. It provides additional reinforcement for word recognition. For example, when deciding how to write a script from a preprimer, the students and teacher reread parts of the text numerous times as they write the scripts on chart tablets.
2. Having the students write a readers theater script from a story can also improve comprehension. The students must decide what important dialogue and narration are necessary to understand the story.
3. Different reading levels can be included in a script to allow readers of varying reading abilities to participate in the same activity.

Further Applications

Basic View of Reading   Reading is an active, reader-based process in which the reader interprets the author's intended meaning through oral interpretative reading.

Patterns of Strengths and Strategies   Readers theater is most appropriate for students who have a dramatic flair and when given the stage will perform. Often a quiet, less verbal student will perform in a readers theater because the expectation is performance.

Learner Patterns That Produce Increased Engagement

1. For a learner who communicates through drama and needs to develop oral reading fluency, this technique is a natural way to develop fluency for this reader.
*2. The highly efficient decoder who is word-bound and does not identify with characters benefits from the naturalness of character identification forced by the readers theater script.
*3. A student who has difficulty tracking develops a purposeful reason to track when reading *short* readers theater scripts.

For Further Reading

Tompkins, G. E. (2004). *Fifty literacy strategies: Step by step* (2nd ed.). Upper Saddle River, NJ: Merrill/Prentice Hall.

Walker, B. J. (2003). *Supporting struggling readers* (2nd ed.). Markham, Ontario: Pippin Publishing Limited.

Reciprocal Teaching

Description   Reciprocal teaching is a technique to develop comprehension of expository text by modeling and practicing how to understand the text. The teacher and students take turns leading a discussion. The teacher provides the initial model by thinking aloud about *how* she constructs a summary, makes up questions, clarifies what is difficult, and predicts what else the text will discuss.

Text   Expository text is preferred.

Predominant Focus of Instruction

1. Processing focus: meaning
2. Instructional phase: during reading
3. Response mode emphasized: oral discussion
4. Strategy emphasized: elaboration
5. Skill emphasized: literal comprehension
6. Source of information: text-based
7. Type of instruction: explicit

Procedure

1. The teacher selects a text from a content area.
2. The teacher explains the four tasks: (a) question generating, (b) summarizing, (c) clarifying the difficult parts, and (d) predicting what the next section will discuss.
3. Both the students and the teacher silently read the first section of the text.
4. The teacher talks about the four tasks of reading for that section.
   a. She constructs several good questions.
   b. She constructs a summary of the section, using the main idea and supporting details.
   c. She clarifies difficult parts by stressing vocabulary and organization.
   d. She predicts what the next section will discuss by using the title and headings.
5. The students help revise the summary, answer the questions, clarify unclear parts of the summary and the text, and evaluate the prediction.
6. After modeling, a student becomes the teacher. He thinks aloud, using the four steps.
7. The teacher becomes a student and assumes the student's role.
8. Students take turns playing "teacher."
9. Periodically the teacher reviews the four activities with students.
   a. Rule for good questions: They should be clear and stand by themselves.
   b. Rule for summaries: Look for the topic sentences, make up a topic sentence if there is none, make lists, and delete what is unimportant.
   c. Rule for clarifying: Look for difficult vocabulary, incomplete information, unclear references, and unusual expressions.

    d. Rule for predictions: Use the title and headings, use questions in the text, and use text structures like *two kinds, four levels*, and so on.
10. As the students play "teacher," the teacher does the following:
    a. She provides feedback about the quality of summaries or questions. When necessary, she models her thinking for the student. For example, she might comment, "That was a start on a summary, but I would summarize by adding . . ."
    b. She provides encouragement to the student playing "teacher." For example, she may say, "I liked the way you identified the important information."

Further Applications

Basic View of Reading Reading is a socio-interactive process in which a reader's interpretation of the text is shaped by discussing ideas with others as well as by the use of the textual and nontextual information. By thinking aloud, the student becomes more aware of how to integrate knowledge sources when reading.

Patterns of Strengths and Strategies Reciprocal teaching is most appropriate for students who have verbal fluency and experiential knowledge of the topics but need to focus their understanding. These students read and retain information, but the complexities of content-area reading often produce an overload of unorganized facts rather than important related information.

Learner Patterns That Produce Increased Engagement

1. A passive yet verbally fluent learner who needs to organize the information rethinks the text by leading the discussion. He also follows the teacher's model.
2. For a sequential learner who tries to memorize a string of unrelated facts rather than focus on the important points and how the facts relate to these points, this technique encourages him to use only the important information in his summary.
*3. For a passive reader who does not monitor information learned, this technique helps him actively summarize text and clarify the difficult parts.

For Further Reading

Gipe, J. P. (2002). *Multiple paths to literacy: Classroom techniques for struggling readers* (5th ed.). Upper Saddle River, NJ: Merrill/Prentice Hall.

Reutzel, D. R., & Cooter, R. (2003). *Strategies for reading assessment and instruction: Helping every child succeed* (2nd ed.). Upper Saddle River, NJ: Merrill/Prentice Hall.

Repeated Readings   *Targeted Reading Levels 1–4*

Description   The repeated readings technique is the oral rereading of a student-selected passage until accuracy and speed are fluent and represent the natural flow of language. Students must be able to read the selection with some degree of accuracy at the beginning of instruction.

Text   Self-selected

Predominant Focus of Instruction

1. Processing focus: print
2. Instructional phase: after reading
3. Response mode emphasized: oral production
4. Strategy emphasized: monitoring
5. Skill emphasized: fluency and word identification
6. Source of information: text-based phasing to reader-based
7. Type of instruction: implicit, but can be adapted to explicit

Procedure

1. The student selects a text he wants to read. The teacher segments the text into manageable passages for oral reading.
2. The teacher makes a copy of the text so she can mark errors as the student reads.
3. The teacher explains that rereading a passage is like practicing a musical instrument or practicing a football play. The repetition helps students read more smoothly and automatically.
4. The student reads the passage orally while the teacher records errors and speed.
5. The errors and speed are charted on a graph.
6. The student practices silently while the teacher listens to other students.
7. The student rereads the passage to the teacher while she records errors with a different-colored pen.
8. The errors and speed are charted on a graph for the second reading. Progress toward the reading goals is discussed.
9. The procedure is continued until a speed of 85 words per minute is reached.
10. Steps 6, 7, and 8 are repeated as needed.

Modifications

1. The teacher can select a text that corresponds to instructional needs.
2. Instead of step 4, the following interventions have been successfully used:
   a. Discussion of the miscues and process of self-correction. The teacher suggests that the student say to himself, "Did that make sense?"
   b. Echo reading (see "Echo Reading") of sentences where the most miscues occur.
   c. Discussion of the author's use of language and intended meaning.

    d. Tape-recording the readings. Then the student listens to the recording, marks errors, and records his time.

3. Only one or two rereadings are used. All readings are charted.

Further Applications

Basic View of Reading   Reading is both a text-based, decoding process and an interactive comprehension process. Comprehension is dependent on the automatic decoding of printed language. Therefore, fluent and accurate decoding are necessary for efficient comprehension. Thus initially, reading is a text-based process.

Patterns of Strengths and Strategies   Repeated readings are most appropriate for students who read word by word and do not use contextual clues to confirm anticipated words as they read. For this learner, the repeated readings encourage the use of overall contextual meaning and sentence structure to predict words and correct mistakes.

Learner Patterns That Produce Increased Engagement

1. For a learner who has a great deal of difficulty with word recognition because of an overemphasis on isolated word drill, this technique uses the overall textual meaning to increase word recognition accuracy.
2. For a learner who cannot blend sounds and must rely, therefore, on the context for word recognition accuracy, this technique, if progressively difficult text is used, allows the student to read more complex text, where words can be recognized by using context rather than what the word looks or sounds like.
*3. For a learner who has become word-bound with heavy phonics instruction and needs to develop fluency and use of contextual cues for word identification, this technique emphasizes using context to identify words rather than sounding out individual words.

For Further Reading

Samuels, S. J. (2002). Reading fluency: Its development and assessment. In A. Farstrup & S. Samuels (Eds.), *What research has to say about reading instruction*. Newark, DE: International Reading Association.

■ *ReQuest*

Description   The ReQuest (reciprocal questioning) technique develops comprehension by having the teacher and the student take turns asking and answering questions. At turning points in the text, the teacher models effective question-asking strategies. The student, in turn, asks appropriate questions by following the model. The goal is to develop self-questioning strategies for the student.

Text   Particularly suited for narrative text but can be used with expository text

Predominant Focus of Instruction

1. Processing focus: meaning
2. Instructional phase: during reading
3. Response mode emphasized: oral discussion
4. Strategy emphasized: prediction and elaboration
5. Skill emphasized: literal and nonliteral comprehension
6. Source of information: reader-based
7. Type of instruction: implicit

Procedure

1. The teacher selects a text that is at the student's reading level and that is predictive in nature.
2. The teacher identifies appropriate points for asking questions.
3. The teacher introduces the ReQuest procedure in terms the student will understand. She tells him that they will be taking turns asking questions about the sentence or paragraph and what it means. The student is to ask questions that a teacher might ask. Then the teacher emphasizes that questions must be answered fully and that they sometimes require support from the text.
4. The student and teacher read the first sentence silently.
5. When the teacher closes her book, the student asks questions. The teacher answers the question, integrating background knowledge and textual information. She also tells how she decided on her answer.
6. Then, the teacher asks questions about any important points not mentioned, modeling integrating information and the predictive nature of the reading by using questions such as "What do you think will happen next? Why do you think so?"
7. The teacher provides feedback about the student's questioning behavior during the procedure.
8. The procedure is used to develop purposes for reading and employs only the first three or four paragraphs.
9. The student reads the rest of the story silently to see whether he answers his questions.
10. Follow-up discussion and activities can be used.

Further Applications

Basic View of Reading Reading is a socio-interactive process in which readers' questioning strategies are shaped by discussing questions with others. This shared thinking requires the reader to monitor his behavior by asking himself questions about the important information in the text and answering these questions, using both textual and nontextual information.

Patterns of Strengths and Strategies The ReQuest procedure is most appropriate for the sequential learner who likes to ask questions but does not always attend to the text for answers. For these students, the approach matches their desire to ask questions, but it focuses on the relevant information in a story and develops an active question-asking role rather than a passive role.

Learner Patterns That Produce Increased Engagement

1. For a learner who asks questions and enjoys breaking a story into parts, reading only sections at a time, this technique uses his strength to show him how to elaborate his understanding using the text and what he knows.
*2. For a learner who asks irrelevant questions when reading and fails to comprehend the main points of the story, this technique focuses his attention on asking important questions and justifying answers.
*3. For a learner who reads words fluently but does not ask himself what the passage means, this technique develops self-questioning and monitoring of comprehension.
*4. For a passive reader who reads words fluently but does not use his prior knowledge to interpret text, this technique asks the student to use both textual and nontextual information to ask and answer questions.

For Further Reading

Gipe, J. P. (2002). *Multiple paths to literacy: Classroom techniques for struggling readers* (5th ed.). Upper Saddle River, NJ: Merrill/Prentice Hall.
Tompkins, G. E. (2004). *Fifty literacy strategies: Step by step* (2nd ed.). Upper Saddle River, NJ: Merrill/Prentice Hall.

■ *Retelling*   *Targeted Reading Levels 1–5*

Description   Retelling is a technique in which a reader makes a mental representation of the story and uses it to orally retell the story. The student tells about the characters, setting, problem, main episodes, and resolution.

Text   Narrative, but can be applied to all kinds

Predominant Focus of Instruction

1. Processing focus: meaning
2. Instructional phase: after reading
3. Response mode emphasized: oral production
4. Strategy emphasized: elaboration
5. Skill emphasized: literal comprehension
6. Source of information: both reader-based and text-based
7. Type of instruction: implicit

Procedure

1. Before reading, the teacher explains to the students that she is going to ask them to retell the story when they have finished reading.
2. If the teacher is expecting the students to include specific information, then she should tell the students before reading.
3. The teacher asks the students to retell the story as if they were telling it to a friend who has never heard it before.
4. The students tell the story, noting the important parts: story setting, theme, plot, sequence, and resolution.
5. If the student is hesitant, the teacher uses prompts at the beginning, middle, and end (see step 6).
6. If the student is unable to tell the story, the retelling is prompted step by step: "Once there was . . . who did . . . in the. . . . (The character) had a problem. . . . To solve the problem, (the character) . . . first . . . second . . . third. . . . Finally, the problem was solved by . . . and then. . . . "
7. When the retelling is complete, the teacher can ask direct questions about important information omitted.
8. The teacher can also refer the student to the text to reread omitted important information.

Modifications

1. Retelling can be enhanced through the use of feltboards, role-playing, and puppets.
2. Retelling can be easily adapted to small-group or partner activities in the classroom.

Further Applications

Basic View of Reading Reading is a socio-interactive process in which the reader reconstructs the story, thinking about what he wants to communicate to the instructional group. His interpretation includes his own perceptions of what is important to remember as well as what he needs to communicate.

Patterns of Strengths and Strategies The retelling approach is most appropriate for students who have verbal strengths and remember the story long enough to internalize it and retell it. Retelling uses their strength to elaborate textual information.

Learner Patterns That Produce Increased Engagement

1. For readers who like to tell stories but fail to recount the most important events in the passage, retelling uses their strength to draw attention to important textual information.
*2. For readers who are hesitant to communicate their ideas, retelling increases the students' confidence by having them practice reformulating the information they read.
*3. For bilingual readers who become confused because they represent text in two language codes, retelling helps these learners use the text and classroom language to express their ideas.

For Further Reading

Glazer, S. M. (1992). *Reading comprehension: Self-monitoring strategies to develop independent readers.* New York: Scholastic.

Morrow, L., & Walker, B. (1977). *The reading team: A handbook for volunteer tutors K–3.* Newark, DE: International Reading Association.

Retrospective Miscue Analysis

Description   The retrospective miscue analysis technique asks the student to listen to his miscues and evaluate the strategies he used as well as the strategies he might have used. In the discussion, the student and teacher discuss what good readers do when they encounter problems when reading.

Text   Stories

Predominant Focus of Instruction

1. Processing focus: print and meaning
2. Instructional phase: during reading
3. Response mode emphasized: oral reading
4. Strategy emphasized: monitoring
5. Skill emphasized: word identification
6. Source of information: reader-based
7. Type of instruction: implicit

Procedure

1. The teacher selects an interesting text that is near the student's instructional level.
2. Before beginning, the teacher conducts a reading interview.
3. The teacher tapes the student reading the selected text.
4. After the initial session, the teacher codes miscues on a printed version of text and preselects miscues to discuss during retrospective miscue analysis.
5. Sometimes, the teacher may want the student to listen to the tape and stop when he hears a miscue.
6. The teacher and student listen to the tape and mark miscues on a printed version of text.
7. The teacher and student discuss miscues using the following questions taken from Goodman and Marek (1996, p. 45):

---

1. Does the miscue make sense?
2. Does the miscue sound like language?
3. a. Was the miscue corrected?
   b. Should it have been?

If the answers to Questions 1 and 3a were "No," then ask:

4. Does the miscue look like what was on the page?
5. Does the miscue sound like what was on the page?

For all miscues, ask:

6. Why do you think you made this miscue?
7. Did that miscue affect your understanding of the text?

---

8. As they discuss, the teacher expands the student's responses by asking, "Why do you think that?" or "How do you know?"

Further Applications

Basic View of Reading Reading is a socio-interactive process in which understanding the process of reading is developed as students explain their thinking about how reading occurs. As students develop an understanding of the reading process, they begin to revalue themselves as readers.

Patterns of Strengths and Strategies Retrospective miscue analysis is most appropriate for students who do not integrate the cueing systems; instead, they rely on a single system for figuring out words. As they evaluate their miscues using the structured questions, they explain how to correct miscues based on more than one cueing system.

Learner Patterns That Produce Increased Engagement

1. For a highly social student who likes to interact with others and discuss his thinking, this technique lets him discuss his strategies for figuring out words.
*2. For a learner who relies heavily on background knowledge when reading without attending to text cues, retrospective miscue analysis encourages him to attend to letters and meaning simultaneously.
*3. For a word-bound reader who does not use his understanding of the passage to correct miscues, this technique helps him talk about how the meaning and words can be used together to read fluently.

For Further Reading

Goodman, Y. M., & Marek, A. M. (1996). Retrospective miscue analysis. In Y. M. Goodman & A. M. Marek (Eds.), *Retrospective miscue analysis: Revaluing readers and reading* (pp. 39–49). Katonah, NY: Richard C. Owen Publishers.

Watson, D., & Hoge, S. (1996). Reader-selected miscues. In Y. M. Goodman & A. M. Marek (Eds.), *Retrospective miscue analysis: Revaluing readers and reading* (pp. 157–164). Katonah, NY: Richard C. Owen Publishers.

■ *Say Something*   *Targeted Reading Levels 2–12*

Description   Say something is a technique to develop personal response to literature by having students take turns saying something at intervals during the reading of the story.

Text   Especially suited for engaging, narrative text but can be applied to all text

Predominant Focus of Instruction

1. Processing focus: meaning
2. Instructional phase: during reading
3. Response mode emphasized: oral discussion
4. Strategy emphasized: elaboration
5. Skill emphasized: nonliteral comprehension
6. Source of information: reader-based
7. Type of instruction: implicit

Procedure

1. The teacher and students choose an engaging text.
2. The teacher demonstrates reading with a partner and making a personal response about the text read.
3. The teacher encourages students to challenge and extend the ideas of their partner.
4. The students choose partners for reading.
5. The partners decide whether the reading will be oral or silent.
6. The partners take turns reading and saying something about what they have read.
7. After the students have finished, the teacher leads a group discussion.
8. The teacher puts a central topic in the middle of an overhead or on the chalkboard.
9. Students generate ideas about the topic and discuss how they fit with the author's ideas.
10. After reading several selections in this fashion, the teacher engages students in a discussion of how they use this strategy as they read.

Further Applications

Basic View of Reading   Reading is a socio-interactive process in which interpretations develop through communicating ideas to others. This sharing enhances and extends text understanding.

Patterns of Strengths and Strategies   The say something technique is appropriate for students who like to talk about what they read as they are reading the text. This dialogue helps social students refine their ideas using their strength.

Learner Patterns That Produce Increased Engagement

1. For a self-directed reader who needs to talk aloud about his personal feelings related to the story, say something allows him to talk about his personal responses to the story.
*2. For a quiet student who needs to verbalize ideas in a safe environment before discussing those ideas in a large group, the say something technique gives him a chance to try out ideas with a partner.

For Further Reading

Short, K. G., Harste, J. C., & Burke, C. (1996). *Creating classrooms for authors and inquirers.* Portsmouth, NH: Heinemann.

Walker, B. J. (2003). *Supporting struggling readers* (2nd ed.). Markham, Ontario: Pippin Publishing Limited.

Shared Reading Approach   *Targeted Reading Levels K–2*

Description   The shared reading approach is for beginning reading instruction that uses the rhythmic, repetitive sentence patterns in young children's stories. The teacher and children read the story together, which creates a predictive set for the words in the story. Then the students read the story by themselves.

Text   Predictable books with patterned language, such as

Run, run, as fast as you can
You can't catch me; I'm the Gingerbread Man.

Predominant Focus of Instruction

1. Processing focus: print
2. Instructional phase: during reading
3. Response mode emphasized: oral
4. Strategy emphasized: prediction and monitoring
5. Skill emphasized: word identification
6. Source of information: reader-based and text-based
7. Type of instruction: implicit

Procedure

1. The teacher chooses a predictable book or story.
2. The teacher and the student talk about the story to develop a predictive set.
3. The student tells what he thinks happens in the story by telling the story page by page, using the pictures. This progression creates a predictive set for the story.
4. The teacher reads the story, letting the student confirm or revise his thinking about what the story is about.
5. The teacher reads the story aloud a second time, inviting the student to read along. She moves her finger above the line of print to mark the flow of language.
6. The teacher continues to read using an oral cloze. The student supplies the missing word in the language pattern.
7. When the student knows the language pattern, he reads the rest of the story on his own.
8. The student reads the whole story again on his own. The teacher assists him when necessary.
9. Using the predictable pattern, the student writes his own story, changing the characters and the setting.

Modification   When the student can predict easily and follows the teacher as she reads, then the teacher can omit steps 3 and 4.

Further Applications

Basic View of Reading   Reading is a socio-interactive process in which readers use their shared understanding as well as language sense to figure out words. Through rhythmic, repetitious language patterns, the student recognizes the printed forms of words and infers the grapho-phonic rule system.

Patterns of Strengths and Strategies   The shared reading approach encourages the student to associate printed words with the predictive patterns of language; therefore, it is most appropriate for students who laboriously try to decode words to derive meaning from text. Because a repetitive sentence pattern is used in this technique, the student can easily predict both what the words are and what they mean at the same time.

Learner Patterns That Produce Increased Engagement

1. For a reader who has facility with verbal language but does not attend to the key features of short similar words found in basal readers, this technique allows him to identify words using the language pattern.
2. For a learner who needs a sense of the whole story before reading, the shared reading approach provides him with a brisk-paced reading of the entire story prior to word identification.
*3. For an extremely slow, laborious letter-by-letter reader, the shared reading approach can restore his sense of the whole and illustrate the predictive nature of reading.
*4. For the learner who reads in a monotone, this approach can restore his sense of rhythm and cadence in reading.

For Further Reading

Short, K. G., Harste, J. C., & Burke, C. (1996). *Creating classrooms for authors and inquirers.* Portsmouth, NH: Heinemann.

Tompkins, G. E. (2004). *Fifty literacy strategies: Step by step* (2nd ed.). Upper Saddle River, NJ: Merrill/Prentice Hall.

■ *Sight Word Approach* *Targeted Reading Levels K–2*

Description The sight word approach is a technique for beginning reading instruction that uses what words mean to develop what the word looks like. Through the use of pictures and oral context, students associate meaning with isolated sight words. These sight words are used to teach decoding.

Text The basic preprimers and primers of published reading series

Predominant Focus of Instruction

1. Processing focus: print
2. Instructional phase: before reading
3. Response mode emphasized: oral discussion
4. Strategy emphasized: prediction
5. Skill emphasized: word identification
6. Source of information: text-based
7. Type of instruction: implicit

Procedure

1. The teacher selects a text that has a controlled sight word vocabulary.
2. She introduces sight words for the story by presenting them in isolation, supplemented by oral context and/or pictures.
3. The teacher reviews the words by placing words on cards and flashing the words in various orders. If the student cannot recall the words, a meaning or semantic prompt is used. If the student cannot recall the word *dog*, the teacher might prompt him by saying, "It rained cats and _____."
4. The student reads the story that contains the words. (The teacher uses the format for directed reading activity or directed reading-thinking activity to direct discussion.)
5. The teacher reinforces sight words by using cloze exercises, games with the word cards, and repetitive reading of stories with the controlled vocabulary.
6. After the student can recognize selected words at sight, the teacher uses analytic phonics (see "Analytic Phonics") to introduce how to decode new words by using analogies to known sight words.

Modifications

1. The teacher can make a word bank by selecting target sight words (including easy words and concrete words) from each lesson and writing them on 3" × 5" cards. On the back of the card, she places the word in a sentence taken from the child's own vocabulary or the story.
2. To reinforce sight word recognition, the teacher can flash the word cards, adding a semantic cue from the story. For example, when the target word *play* is forgotten, the teacher uses the semantic cue, "We like to run and _____."

3. The teacher uses the word cards to form a word bank that can be used to write and combine sentences. This bank becomes a spelling dictionary of known words for writing during uninterrupted sustained silent writing.
4. Students classify the word cards according to categories and make a feature analysis grid (see "Feature Analysis Grid").
5. The teacher constructs word sorts (see "Word Sorts").

Further Applications

Basic View of Reading   Reading is a text-based process in which the reader learns the words in the text before he reads the story. As he learns the words, he associates their meaning in oral context. Therefore, learning to read is a process of accumulating enough words recognized at sight that a student can decode new words in a story by using the written context and decoding analogies. Initially, this approach places a high demand on visual feature analysis and phonemic segmentation.

Patterns of Strengths and Strategies   The sight word approach is most appropriate for students who have developed a systematic way of analyzing the key visual features of words.

Learner Patterns That Produce Increased Engagement

1. A learner who attends to the key features of words notices what visual features are alike and what visual features are different. Presenting the word with a semantic cue helps the student focus on meaning and visual cues at the same time.
*2. For an inattentive learner who attends more to the pictures and context when reading stories than the important features of the words, the sight word approach isolates the word so the student can identify and remember the key visual features.
*3. For a passive learner who needs direct instruction in how to select the key features so he can remember what the words look like, the sight word approach provides a tool for the teacher to talk about what words look like.

For Further Reading

Gipe, J. P. (2002). *Multiple paths to literacy: Classroom techniques for struggling readers* (5th ed.). Upper Saddle River, NJ: Merrill/Prentice Hall.
Rasinski, T., & Padak, N. (2001). *From phonics to fluency: Effective teaching of decoding and reading fluency in the elementary school.* Boston, MA: Allyn & Bacon.

Sound Boxes   *Targeted Reading Levels 1–4*

Description   Sound boxes is a technique to develop print processing. The student writes a sentence by slowly saying the words. The student thinks about the letter sounds and then writes the letters in the words.

Text   Student-generated

Predominant Focus of Instruction

1. Processing focus: print
2. Instructional phase: after reading
3. Response mode emphasized: written and oral production
4. Strategy emphasized: prediction and monitoring
5. Skill emphasized: word identification
6. Source of information: reader-based information
7. Type of instruction: implicit

Procedure

1. The teacher provides a blank writing book with each page divided in half. The top half is for practice writing, and the bottom half is for sentence writing.
2. Assisted by the teacher, the student composes a brief message (one or two sentences).
3. The sentence is written word by word.
4. If the student is unfamiliar with the printed form of a word, he uses the practice section of the page.
5. The teacher assists by drawing boxes for each letter of the unfamiliar word. For example, the word *dog* would look like this:

6. The student slowly says the sounds and places the letters he knows in the appropriate boxes.

7. The teacher supplies any unknown letters in the appropriate boxes, slowly saying the sounds in the word. In the example, the teacher places an *o* in the middle box and says, "d-d-o-o-g-g-."
8. The teacher asks, "Does this look right?"
9. The student evaluates the word and writes it in his sentence.

10. After the sentence is written, the teacher writes it on a sentence strip and then cuts it apart into words.
11. The student reconstructs the sentence, matching the words in his writing book.
12. The sentence is always read in its entirety.

Modifications

1. When a word is unfamiliar to the student, the teacher may want to use magnetic letters before having the student use the writing book. In that case, the student constructs a familiar part and then the teacher supplies other letters.
2. The teacher may use this technique when editing writing during classroom activities.

Further Applications

Basic View of Reading   Reading is an active, reader-based process in which the reader predicts what words will look like by using his understanding of the grapho-phonic system (sound segmentation and sound synthesis).

Patterns of Strengths and Strategies   The sound boxes approach is most appropriate for students who write with facility and can predict some letters in a word. By predicting and writing the letters, the student creates his own system for recognizing words.

Learner Patterns That Produce Increased Engagement

*1. For a learner who uses only what he knows when comprehending text and therefore guesses wildly when he comes to an unknown word, sound boxes help this student focus on the details of printed words as he writes a word.
*2. For the passive learner who does not attempt to figure out unknown words, the student actively predicts letters in words by using sound boxes.

For Further Reading

Fountas, I. C., & Pinnell, G. S. (1996). *Guided reading: Good first teaching for all children.* Portsmouth, NH: Heinemann.
Gunning, T. G. (1998). *Assessing and correcting reading and writing difficulties.* Boston: Allyn & Bacon.

Story Drama

Description   Story drama is a method for developing reading comprehension by using the natural dramatic abilities of students. The students think about how a story will end by role-playing scenes from a story that they have read up to a certain point. By taking the roles of the various characters, the students use their knowledge of similar experiences, their affective response to the characters, and key information to act out their interpretation of the story.

Text   Various kinds of literature. Picture storybooks and adventure stories with an intriguing plot lend themselves to dramatic interpretation.

Predominant Focus of Instruction

1. Processing focus: meaning
2. Instructional phase: during reading
3. Response mode emphasized: oral and kinesthetic
4. Strategy emphasized: prediction and monitoring
5. Skill emphasized: nonliteral comprehension
6. Source of information: reader-based
7. Type of instruction: implicit

Procedure

1. The teacher selects a story with an intriguing plot.
2. The teacher or the students read until they have enough information about the characters to role-play the story.
3. The teacher assigns the students the character roles from the story.
4. The teacher uses key props to engage the students in the drama in a concrete way.
5. The teacher and the students begin the drama at the point of interruption.
6. The students dramatize their predictions through role-playing.
7. In the process of the dramatization, the teacher may stop the drama and have students exchange roles.
8. The students discuss their predictions and the information used to make them.
9. After the dramatization, students write an ending for the story.
10. Finally, the students finish reading the story.
11. The students discuss and compare both the drama and the story ending.
12. The teacher and students discuss their personal interpretations evidenced in the drama and how their individual viewpoints influence those interpretations.

Further Applications

Basic View of Reading   Reading is a socio-interactive process in which the roles students play in the drama shape their personal interpretation and the group interaction focuses their comprehension. Reading requires a personal identification with the story's characters, problems, and events; therefore, the affective purposes of the reader and situational variables influence his model of meaning.

Patterns of Strengths and Strategies   Story drama is most appropriate for students who are extremely expressive, divergent, and simultaneous when thinking. For these students, the powerful influence of personal, kinesthetic imagery is used to analyze the constructive process. This strategy encourages active involvement in analyzing not only the story line and character development but also the effect that personal identification with story characters has on comprehension.

Learner Patterns That Produce Increased Engagement

1. For a student who prefers to use dramatic expression and body language to communicate, instead of words, story drama uses this strength to aid the student in verbally communicating his ideas about the story.
2. For the dramatic, impulsive learner who needs to attend to the important information in the text, story drama focuses his attention on character traits and story theme in order to portray a character.
*3. For a learner who relies too heavily on personal identification with story characters, story drama helps him analyze how his personal identification affects his interpretation.
*4. For a passive learner who needs to engage in active interpretation of the story line, story drama concretely demonstrates how to be actively involved in a story.

For Further Reading

Cunningham, P. M., & Allington, R. L. (2003). *Classrooms that work: They can all read and write* (3rd ed.). New York: Longman.
Short, K. G., Harste, J. C., & Burke, C. (1996). *Creating classrooms for authors and inquirers.* Portsmouth, NH: Heinemann.

■ *Story Mapping*   *Targeted Reading Levels 1–8*

Description   Story mapping is a visual representation of the logical sequence of events in a narrative text. The elements of setting, problem, goal, events, and resolution are recorded visually on a sheet of paper.

Text   Any narrative text with a fairly coherent story line

Predominant Focus of Instruction

1. Processing focus: meaning
2. Instructional phase: during or after reading
3. Response mode emphasized: written
4. Strategy emphasized: monitoring and elaboration
5. Skill emphasized: literal comprehension
6. Source of information: text-based
7. Type of instruction: explicit

Procedure

1. The teacher selects a narrative passage of sufficient length so that it has a cohesive story line.
2. The teacher prepares questions to lead students through the story map.
3. The teacher discusses the organization of a story by explaining that every story has a beginning, middle, and end.
   a. The beginning tells the place and who the characters are.
   b. During the middle of the story, the central character has a problem and makes a plan to solve it. Certain events in the story lead to solving the problem.
   c. The end of the story tells how the character(s) solved the problem.
4. The teacher explains the visual story map (see the accompanying figure) and relates it to story organization.
5. The students read the story.
6. The teacher and students fill out the map together. The teacher uses the prepared questions to guide the completion of the map.
7. The teacher and students compare this story with other stories they have read.

Further Applications

Basic View of Reading   Reading is an interactive process in which the reader's understanding of the elements of a story affects interpretation of the story.

Patterns of Strengths and Strategies   Story mapping is most appropriate for the learner who profits from a visual representation of story organization to develop adequate comprehension. Often the abundance of facts overwhelms the young

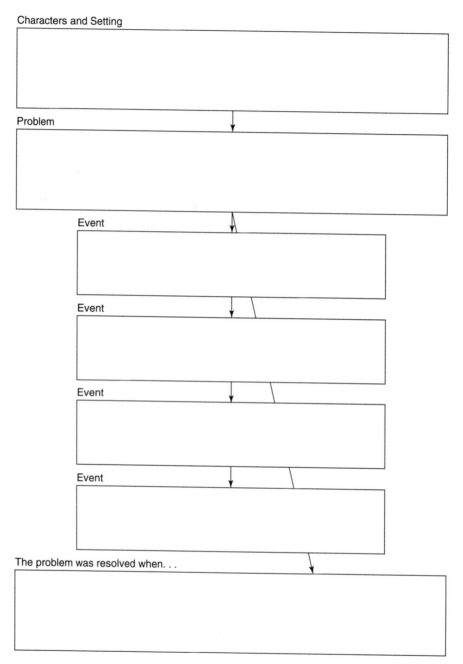

Characters and Setting

Problem

Event

Event

Event

Event

The problem was resolved when. . .

STORY MAPPING

reader, who needs a simple structure such as a story map to apply to stories to help him organize and remember events.

Learner Patterns That Produce Increased Engagement

1. For a learner who thinks in visual images but who has difficulty organizing sequential events of the story and remembering factual detail, the story map uses his visual strengths to develop the text-based skill of story development.
*2. For the passive learner who has difficulty retelling the story and often leaves out key events or characters in the retelling, the story map gives a structure to the retelling and reasons for the facts to be remembered.
*3. For the fact-bound learner who lacks a cohesive sense of story, the map provides him with an overall view of the story.

For Further Reading

Gipe, J. P. (2002). *Multiple paths to literacy: Classroom techniques for struggling readers* (5th ed.). Upper Saddle River, NJ: Merrill/Prentice Hall.

Story Writing Approach

Targeted Reading Levels 3–6,
but can be used at all levels

Description Story writing is an instructional format for teaching narrative writing that includes three stages: prewriting, writing, and evaluating. By writing their own stories, students increase their awareness of story parts.

Text Student's own writing

Predominant Focus of Instruction

1. Processing focus: meaning
2. Instructional phase: after reading
3. Response mode emphasized: written discourse
4. Strategy emphasized: elaboration
5. Skill emphasized: nonliteral comprehension
6. Source of information: reader-based
7. Type of instruction: implicit

Procedure

1. The teacher introduces the structure of a story. Stories have a beginning (the characters and place), middle (problems and the events), and an end (solution of the problem).
2. The teacher and the students brainstorm ideas to select a topic and information that might go into the story.
3. Using the information collected, the students write their stories. The teacher emphasizes that the story needs to flow from one idea to the next and make sense.
4. The teacher has the students reread their stories to see whether they make sense. She uses the following questions:
   a. Does the story make sense?
   b. Do I have all the story parts?
   c. Have I left out any information that the reader might need to know in order to understand my story?
5. The students revise any unclear information.
6. The students make a final copy of their stories.

Modifications

1. In prewriting, students can use a visual story map to form the outline of the story.
2. For the student who has a great deal of difficulty, the teacher might use a story frame with only minimal ideas deleted.
3. Guided imagery journeys may be used as a prewriting activity.
4. A story can be composed by a small group of students. Each person writes a segment of the story and then passes the text to the next person. Each student's contribution to the story line must build upon prior information and make sense.
5. Pairs of students can read and edit each other's stories.
6. Instead of step 4, the students can take their stories to the author's chair where students provide input on the three questions.

Further Applications

Basic View of Reading   Reading is an active, reader-based process in which the reader interprets the author's intended meaning. An author writes a text that allows a clear interpretation by the reader but assumes that a certain amount of inferencing will occur on the part of the reader.

Patterns of Strengths and Strategies   The story writing approach is most appropriate for students who need to write in order to experience how a story is organized so that it makes sense. This approach emphasizes the constructive nature of reading and that the text needs to "make sense."

Learner Patterns That Produce Increased Engagement

1. For the learner who writes and reads for self-understanding and meaning but does not realize that a story is a contractual agreement between reader and writer, this technique helps him think about what the author wants him to understand.
*2. The passive learner who does not understand story organization learns to attend to story features when he reads by writing his own parts of a story.
*3. The reader who relies on his own background knowledge to interpret text and does not attend to sentence meaning becomes more sensitive to the function that text structure has in developing meaning by writing his own stories and listening to others interpret them.

For Further Reading

DeCarlo, J. E. (1995). *Perspectives in whole language.* Boston: Allyn & Bacon.

Short, K. G., Harste, J. C., & Burke, C. (1996). *Creating classrooms for authors and inquirers.* Portsmouth, NH: Heinemann.

■ *Summarization*   *Targeted Reading Levels 6–12*

Description   Summarization teaches the student how to write summaries of what he reads. He is shown how to delete unimportant information, group similar ideas, decide on or invent topic sentences, and list supporting details. These procedures culminate in a short paragraph that reflects the most important information.

Text   Most appropriate for expository text

Predominant Focus of Instruction

1. Processing focus: meaning
2. Instructional phase: after reading
3. Response mode emphasized: written discourse
4. Strategy emphasized: elaboration
5. Skill emphasized: literal comprehension
6. Source of information: text-based to reader-based
7. Type of instruction: explicit

Procedure

1. The teacher selects an expository text.
2. She describes a summary as a short version of the text that contains all the important information.
3. The teacher explains that the purpose of writing summaries is to put all the important information together so it can be remembered better.
4. The students read the selection and ask themselves, "What is this mainly about?"
5. The teacher reads her summary of the selection and presents it on the overhead.
6. In the text, students mark the information the teacher used in the summary.
7. The teacher talks about the rules for writing summaries by telling students how she wrote her summary.
8. The teacher demonstrates the rule of deleting trivial information. She points out that many writers tell us interesting information that is not a key idea. She tells them to ignore this information when writing a summary.
9. The teacher demonstrates the rule for deleting repeated information. She explains that many writers repeat information to make their point. When writing a summary, students should use an idea only once and ignore repeated information.
10. The teacher demonstrates the rule for combining details into a generalization. When possible, students should combine details that fit into the same category and rename that category with a bigger category. For example, *pigs, horses, cows,* and *chickens* can be renamed to *farm animals.*
11. The teacher demonstrates how to select the topic sentence. She points out that the topic sentence is the author's one sentence summary. It usually comes at the beginning or the end of the paragraph.

12. The teacher demonstrates how to invent a topic sentence when a paragraph has no summary sentence. In this case, she shows how to organize all the important information into one category. Then she writes a sentence that tells what the paragraph is mainly about. She shows how to think about the important information and relate it.
13. The students write a summary for the demonstration selection and check their summaries individually against the rules.
14. The students compare their summaries in small groups.
15. The students write a summary for another selection.
16. When finished, the students describe how they constructed their summaries.
17. The teacher shows them her summary for the same selection and talks about how she constructed it.
18. The students write summaries for several more selections on their own.

Further Applications

Basic View of Reading   Reading is an interactive process in which the reader decides what is important about the text in order to summarize what it says.

Patterns of Strengths and Strategies   Summarization is most appropriate for students who like to think about what a text says but have difficulty remembering the facts that support this main point. The approach helps these students focus on relating all the textual information that is important to the key idea.

Learner Patterns That Produce Increased Engagement

*1. For a reader who quickly reduces information to the main ideas but needs to write out some important details to support the main idea, this technique helps the reader understand how details relate to main points.
*2. For a reader who cannot tie important information together in order to remember information, summarization helps him decide on general categories that relate details.
*3. For a reader who thinks everything in the text is important, summarization helps him learn to delete unimportant and repeated information.

For Further Reading
John, J. L., & Lenski, S. (2001). *Improving reading: A handbook of strategies* (3rd. ed.). Dubuque, IA: Kendall/Hunt.

■ *Summary Experience Approach*   *Targeted Reading Levels K–3*

Description The student and teacher talk about the story the class is currently reading. Based on the classroom reading material, the student is asked to retell the classroom story while the teacher records or writes down the retelling. This summary (dictated retelling) becomes material that is read by the student.

Text Classroom stories

Predominant Focus of Instruction

1. Processing focus: print and meaning
2. Instructional phase: after listening
3. Response mode emphasized: oral retelling
4. Strategy emphasized: prediction and monitoring
5. Skill emphasized: word identification and literal comprehension
6. Source of information: reader-based and text-based
7. Type of instruction: implicit

Procedure

1. The teacher engages the students in dialogue about the selection being read in the classroom, asking the student to relate the key ideas.
2. The students are asked to retell the classroom selection while the teacher serves as a secretary and writes down what the students say, which becomes a written summary that the students read.
3. Using leading questions, the teacher guides the student to retell the selection by using questions such as: What happened next? Who are the characters? How does the story end? (For additional prompts, see "Retelling" in this part.)
4. The students and teacher read the summary together to revise any unclear statements or phrases. The summary follows the natural language pattern of the students.
5. The teacher and students read the summary repeatedly so that the repetition of the summary helps each student recognize the words in the summary and the words in the classroom story.
6. Retype the summary and make several copies. Let the students take one copy home to practice.
7. Create a book of story summaries.

Modification The teacher can use a story map before the retelling to help the students dictate the summary.

Further Applications

Basic View of Reading Reading is an active, reader-based process. By reading his own summary, the student will learn key vocabulary words. Because the summary is short and uses his own language structure, the student will be able to remember the words in the summary, which will in turn facilitate understanding the classroom story.

Patterns of Strengths and Strategies   The summary experience approach is most appropriate for students who have facility with language and are reader-based thinkers. If the student uses his own language to retell the story rather than the exact words in the text, then the summary experience matches his own way of expressing and interpreting meaning; therefore, this technique facilitates word learning by asking the student to identify words using his own interpretation of the story.

Learner Patterns That Produce Increased Engagement

1. For a reader who readily thinks of the main ideas in the story and can retell a story with ease, the summary experience approach uses the student's strength (thinking of the main actions) to facilitate word identification.
2. For an extremely verbal student whose verbalization, at times, interferes with focusing on the words in the text, the summary experience approach uses this strength to facilitate recognizing individual words.
*3. A student who needs to improve comprehension will be able to use his own language to understand the story rather than answer direct questions posed by the teacher.

For Further Reading

Reutzel, D. R., & Cooter, R. (2003). *Strategies for reading assessment and instruction: Helping every child succeed* (2nd ed.). Upper Saddle River, NJ: Merrill/Prentice Hall.
Walker, B. (2003). *Supporting struggling readers* (2nd ed.). Markham, Ontario: Pippin Publishing Limited.

■ **Synthetic (Explicit) Phonics**   *Targeted Reading Levels 1–2*

Description Synthetic phonics teaches sound-symbol relationships (rules) in words to facilitate word identification. The student is systematically instructed to say the letter sounds in words and then blend the sounds together to decode the unknown word. The rapid transfer of decoding principles to new words is expected as the text includes many words that follow the rule.

Text Decodable words and some isolated drill

Predominant Focus of Instruction

1. Processing focus: print
2. Instructional phase: before reading
3. Response mode emphasized: oral discussion
4. Strategy emphasized: elaboration
5. Skill emphasized: word analysis
6. Source of information: text-based
7. Type of instruction: explicit

Procedure

1. The teacher selects phonic rules to be taught.
2. She selects texts and words to illustrate the rule.
3. The teacher directly teaches the letter sounds.

   The letter *s* goes "*s-s-s.*"

   The letter *t* goes "*t-t-t.*"

   The letter *n* goes "*n-n-n.*"

   The letter *m* goes "*m-m-m.*"

   In short words that have a consonant at the beginning and the end and an *a* in the middle, the letter *a* says "*a-a-a.*"

4. The student blends the sounds together to form words.

   S-a-m says "*Sam.*"

   S-a-t says "*sat.*"

5. The student reads the words in a text that uses the sound-symbol relationships the teacher has introduced.

   Sam is on the mat.

   The man is on the mat.

   Sam sat on the man on the mat.

6. The teacher facilitates the transfer of rules to new words. In the example, she teaches the sounds for *d, h,* and *c.* Then she asks the student to read:

The man has a hat. The hat is in the sand.

Sam is a cat. Sam ran in the sand.

Sam ran to the man.

Sam sat on the man's hat.

The man is mad at Sam. Sam ran.

Further Applications

Basic View of Reading Reading is a text-based process in which effective reading is based on accurate decoding of words. Learning sounds of letters and sounding out words precedes reading stories; therefore, decoding precedes comprehension.

Patterns of Strengths and Strategies Synthetic phonics is a process of successive blending of sounds, requiring the child to hold a sequence of sounds in her memory while synthesizing them to form a word. Young children who have facility with sound blending and can hold oral sequences in memory will have the greatest success with this method.

Learner Patterns That Produce Increased Engagement

1. For a learner who has facility with language so that the systematic decoding of words becomes a tool rather than an end by itself, the phonics approach facilitates word identification without interfering with fluency.
*2. For a learner who can blend sounds and profits from direct instruction in the sound system, this technique directly shows him how to decode new words and directs his attention to individual letters.
*3. The learner who can blend sounds but has no visual memory can always decode the word he has forgotten.

For Further Reading

McCormick, S. (2003). *Instructing students who have literacy problems* (4th ed.). Upper Saddle River, NJ: Merrill/Prentice Hall.

Snow, C. E., Burns, M. S., & Griffin, P. (1998). *Preventing reading difficulties in young children.* Washington, DC: National Academy Press.

Talking Books   *Targeted Reading Levels K–5*

Description   The talking books method uses tape-recorded readings of selected stories to increase word recognition and reading fluency. The student repeatedly reads along with a tape until he can read the text fluently with comprehension.

Text   Stories with specially prepared tape recordings

Predominant Focus of Instruction

1. Processing focus: print
2. Instructional phase: during reading
3. Response mode emphasized: oral
4. Strategy emphasized: prediction
5. Skill emphasized: word identification and fluency
6. Source of information: reader-based
7. Type of instruction: implicit

Procedure

1. The student selects a text that is interesting to him.
2. The teacher secures or makes a tape recording of the story.
3. If she makes a tape, she includes the following:
   a. She segments the story so that the student can easily finish a tape in one sitting.
   b. She cues the page numbers so the student can easily find the page.
   c. She records the text, using the natural phrases of language.
4. The student follows the line of print with his finger.
5. The student listens to the tape recording to develop an overall understanding of the story.
6. Then the student listens and reads along with the tape as many times as necessary until he can read the text fluently.
7. The student rehearses the text by himself.
8. The student reads the text to the teacher.
9. The teacher evaluates fluency and comprehension.
10. If the student reads the passage fluently with comprehension, he listens and reads the next segment of the story or another story.

Further Applications

Basic View of Reading   Reading is a reader-based process in which the reader's personal understanding of the story drives the word recognition process. By repeatedly listening to the story, the reader gains an understanding of the story meaning, story structure, and sentence structure. He uses this understanding to facilitate word recognition in the story.

Patterns of Strengths and Strategies   The talking books technique is most appropriate for the beginning reader or the nonfluent reader who easily memorizes stories. This memorization facilitates fluent reading of text and allows the student to attend to both meaning and print simultaneously. By memorizing stories, the student is exposed to lots of words in context, enabling him to apply phonic knowledge, recognize sight words, and self-correct as he meaningfully reads text.

Learner Patterns That Produce Increased Engagement

1. A learner who relies too heavily on background knowledge when orally reading does not self-correct using graphic cues. This technique develops word identification by using the overall textual meaning (a strength) to identify words.
2. For a passive reader who reads word by word without attention to meaning, this technique restores reading for meaning by having the student learn to read whole stories with expression and by allowing the student to experience success.
*3. A nonfluent reader who has had an overemphasis of synthetic or explicit phonic instruction has become word-bound. This technique develops reading in meaningful phrases.
*4. For a slow reader who has not developed either decoding skills or a recognition vocabulary, talking books use memorizing whole stories so that the student can read lots of words before developing either phonic knowledge or a sight word vocabulary.

For Further Reading

Rasinski, T., & Padak, N. (2004). *Effective reading strategies: Teaching children who find reading difficult* (3rd ed.). Upper Saddle River, NJ: Merrill/Prentice Hall.

Walker, B. J. (2003). *Supporting struggling readers* (2nd ed.). Markham, Ontario: Pippin Publishing Limited.

▌ *Thematic Experience Approach*   *Targeted Reading Levels 4–12*

Description   The thematic experience approach is a technique to develop an in-depth knowledge of a particular topic through integrating reading and writing activities.

Text   Particularly suited for expository text, but can be used with all types

Predominant Focus of Instruction

1. Processing focus: meaning
2. Instructional phase: before and after reading
3. Response mode emphasized: oral discussion and written responses
4. Strategy emphasized: elaboration
5. Skill emphasized: literal and nonliteral comprehension
6. Source of information: text-based leading to reader-based
7. Type of instruction: implicit

Procedure

1. The teacher and students select a topic to be studied.
2. The teacher creates experiences to engage students in a general understanding of the topic.
3. The teacher and students then discuss what they are learning and already know about the topic.
4. The teacher and students brainstorm possible research topics while the teacher records these on a chart on chalkboard.
5. The students select a possible research topic and discuss it in a small group.
6. The teacher discusses research focus with each student, elaborating ideas and suggesting possible reference sources.
7. Each student independently researches his special focus related to the topic.
8. Each student takes notes on his special focus area.
9. Each student prepares a presentation on his special focus to share with the class. This presentation can take many response modes: graphic organizer, video, written report, and so on.
10. The teacher and students evaluate their learning.

Further Applications

Basic View of Reading   Reading is an active, reader-based process in which students build topic knowledge, using what they know. What they know is usually related to their individual interests.

Patterns of Strengths and Strategies   The thematic experience approach is appropriate for students who build experiences by pursuing their own interests. In researching their interests, these students build a network of new concepts.

Learner Patterns That Produce Increased Engagement

1. For readers who prefer to research topics independently to expand their knowledge, the thematic experience approach allows them to build their own theories and concepts.
*2. For readers who have little prior knowledge about a topic, the thematic experience approach begins by using interest to build a network of ideas on an unknown topic.
*3. For bilingual readers who need to build a network of language to express concepts, the thematic experience approach allows them to make connections in both language codes during the experience.

For Further Reading

Short, K. G., Harste, J. C., & Burke, C. (1996). *Creating classrooms for authors and inquirers*. Portsmouth, NH: Heinemann.

Think-Aloud Approach

Targeted Reading Levels:
All levels, but most appropriate for 4–12

Description   The think-aloud approach uses the student's thinking to develop active reading. By following the sequence of self-directed questions, the student learns to monitor his understanding as he reads.

Text   Narrative text is most appropriate.

Predominant Focus of Instruction

1. Processing focus: meaning
2. Instructional phase: during reading
3. Response mode emphasized: oral discussion
4. Strategy emphasized: prediction and monitoring
5. Skill emphasized: nonliteral comprehension
6. Source of information: reader-based
7. Type of instruction: initially explicit, but moves rapidly to implicit

Procedure

1. The teacher decides to think aloud about the active process of predicting and revising a model of meaning.
2. The teacher selects a text that is at the appropriate level and that has a fairly cohesive story line.
3. She decides on key prediction points.
4. The teacher begins by modeling how to think through the story. She asks herself:

   "What must I do? . . . I must guess what the author is going to say. . . . A good strategy is to use the title. . . . From the title, I bet that . . . "

5. Using another section of the story, the teacher models her plan for betting:

   "Now, let's see what's my plan for betting. . . . To make my bet, I already know that. . . . To prove my bet, I must look for hints in the text . . . "

6. The teacher writes these two aspects on a chalkboard:

   "I already know. . . . Hints from the text . . . "

7. Using another section, the teacher answers the question: Does my guess make sense?

   "I wonder how it fits? . . . It fits because _____."

8. Using other sections of the story, the teacher writes "oops" on the chalkboard while she models her correction strategies by saying:

   "Oops, that doesn't make sense. . . . I need to check my thinking. . . . So far, I'm right about . . . but wrong about . . . "

9. As she models this strategy, she also models her self-talk related to making a mistake by saying:

"It's okay to make a mistake. . . . I can change my bet as I get more information. From the new information, I bet that . . . or I wonder whether . . . "

10. Using another section, she models her tentative thinking by saying, "Hmmmm" and writing it on the chalkboard and saying:

"Hmmm. Sometimes, I am just not sure. . . . Maybe it's . . . or maybe it's . . . "

11. The teacher models confirming her predictions by saying, *"I knew it, that sure fits. . . . So far I'm right!"*
12. She writes, "I knew it" on the chalkboard. On the chalkboard, the phrases for revision are written like the following:

Ooops!   Hmmm.   I knew it!
13. The student reads another example passage, talking aloud and using steps 4–12.
14. When comprehension breaks down, the teacher models her own thinking rather than asking questions. She says, "When I read that I thought . . . "

Further Applications

Basic View of Reading   Reading is an interactive process in which the reader builds a model of meaning based on textual and nontextual information. As the reader builds his model of meaning, he predicts, monitors, and elaborates.

Patterns of Strengths and Strategies   The think-aloud approach is most appropriate for students who overrely on what they know, failing to monitor reading comprehension. For these students, the approach matches their strength of prior knowledge and helps them revise their understanding based on textual information.

Learner Patterns That Produce Increased Engagement

1. For a learner who does not use self-talk to monitor the sources of information used to construct his answers, this technique encourages the internal dialogue that accompanies effective comprehension.
*2. For a passive learner who needs to actively engage in forming and revising his interpretations of the text, this technique gives him a plan for thinking and checking his understanding.
*3. For a learner who knows the meanings of words but depends on teacher questioning to interpret the important information in the text, this technique gives him the steps to develop his own questions.

For Further Reading

Roskos, K., & Walker, B. J. (1994). *Interactive handbook for understanding reading diagnosis.* Upper Saddle River, NJ: Merrill/Prentice Hall.
Wilhelm, J. D. (2001). *Improving comprehension think-aloud strategies: Modeling what good readers do.* New York: Scholastic.

Vocabulary Self-Collection Strategy   *Target Reading Levels: All levels*

Description   The vocabulary self-collection strategy (VSS) is a technique for developing word meanings by having small groups of students select words they would like to study and tell why they are important to a topic of study.

Text   Selected vocabulary words from a text that has been read by all students

Predominant Focus of Instruction

1. Processing focus: meaning
2. Instructional phase: after reading
3. Response mode emphasized: oral discussion
4. Strategy emphasized: elaboration
5. Skill emphasized: word meaning
6. Source of information: reader-based and text-based
7. Type of instruction: implicit

Procedure

1. After reading a selected passage, the teacher organizes students into groups of four or five students each.
2. The student groups are to find at least two words they would like to study.
3. In their groups, the students describe the following about words each member would like to study:
   a. Demonstrate where they found the words in the passage.
   b. Discuss what they think the word might mean.
   c. Discuss why the word is important to them.
4. The small groups prioritize the words they would like to study.
5. Each group nominates a word that has not been previously listed with the reasons for learning in a total class discussion.
6. The total class refines definitions and, if necessary, selects words for further study.
7. Students record the final word list along with personalized definitions in their vocabulary journals.
8. Students revisit their new words, using extension activities such as a feature analysis grid (see "Feature Analysis Grid" in this part).

Further Applications

Basic View of Reading   Reading is a socio-interactive process in which readers' definitional knowledge is shaped by group members' understanding as well as their personal understanding.

Patterns of Strengths and Strategies The vocabulary self-collection strategy encourages the student to use not only his experiences but also the experiences of his peers to expand his definitional knowledge; therefore, it is most appropriate for students who share and rely on their social interactions for learning. This strategy facilitates learning for these students because it allows students to converse about what and how they are learning.

Learner Patterns That Produce Increased Engagement

1. For a highly verbal learner who likes learning through incidental learning, this technique allows him to use the nuances of personal language to develop definitional knowledge.
2. For a highly social learner who likes to learn from his peers in the classroom, this technique allows him to learn word meanings as he talks with others in the classroom.
*3. For a learner who needs to use his personal interest to develop word meanings because previous word learning experiences resulted in negative attributions toward vocabulary development, vocabulary self-collection offers a group setting to share interests.

For Further Reading

Gipe, J. P. (2002). *Multiple paths to literacy: Classroom techniques for struggling readers* (5th ed.). Upper Saddle River, NJ: Merrill/Prentice Hall.

Ruddell, M. R. (2005). *Teaching content reading and writing* (4th ed.). Hoboken, NJ: Wiley Publishers.

■ *Webbing*   *Targeted Reading Levels: All levels*

Description   This technique develops word meanings by visually mapping the relationships among words. The target concept is placed in the center of the web. Related concepts are arranged around this concept to show relationships between what the student already knows and the new concept.

Text   Key concepts; often used to introduce vocabulary words for a story

Predominant Focus of Instruction

1. Processing focus: meaning
2. Instructional phase: before or after reading
3. Response mode emphasized: oral discussion and written responses
4. Strategy emphasized: elaboration
5. Skill emphasized: nonliteral comprehension
6. Source of information: reader-based
7. Type of instruction: implicit

Procedure

1. The teacher chooses a concept that is a key element of what is to be read.
2. She places the word inside a circle in the middle of a blank page or chalkboard.
3. The students and the teacher brainstorm what is already known about this concept and place the information in conceptual relationships, making a visual array of the relationships.
4. The teacher adds each new concept or word that describes the central concept to the web by drawing lines and new circles that indicate their relationships (see the accompanying figure).
5. The students read the story.
6. The students and the teacher add additional story information to the web.
7. The students and the teacher discuss new understandings to known concepts and new relationships that were gained by reading.

Modification   For narrative text, character webs can be developed using the attributes of the main character. This technique is useful when reading chapter books.

Further Applications

Basic View of Reading   Reading is an interactive process in which readers use their background knowledge to create web relationships between word knowledge (verbal labels) and world knowledge (concepts).

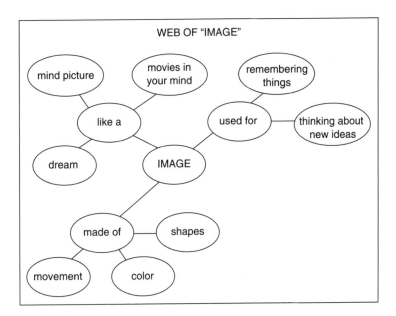

WEB

Patterns of Strengths and Strategies Webbing encourages the student to use his experiential knowledge to expand his definitional knowledge; therefore, it is most appropriate for the student who tends to think visually about the relationship of information without describing these relationships in words.

Learner Patterns That Produce Increased Engagement

1. For a reader who perceives visual-spatial relationships rather than definitional relationships, this technique helps the student use his visual understanding of relationships to increase his comprehension.
2. For a bilingual student who has a well-developed conceptual base but needs development of word knowledge, the visual webbing of relationships helps him make specific comparisons between the events of his life and the words that are commonly used to express them.
*3. For a student with verbal weaknesses who needs to develop word conceptual knowledge in order to read and understand, this technique helps him develop conceptual relationships among words as well as the verbal labels used to express those relationships.

For Further Reading
Bromley, K. D. (1996). *Webbing with literature: Creating story maps with children's books* (2nd ed.). Boston: Allyn & Bacon.

■ *Word Analogy Strategy* *Targeted Reading Levels 1–4*

Description Word analogy strategy is an approach to teaching phonics in which children are taught a strategic process of using word patterns they know to figure out unfamiliar words.

Text Individual words

Predominant Focus of Instruction

1. Processing focus: print
2. Instructional phase: skill lesson
3. Response mode emphasized: oral
4. Strategy emphasized: monitoring
5. Skill emphasized: word identification and word analysis
6. Source of information: text-based
7. Type of instruction: explicit

Procedure

1. The teacher explains that sometimes individuals use words they know to figure out unfamiliar words.
2. The teacher models how to find familiar letter patterns in unfamiliar words. For instance, when reading the word *stain,* the student could identify *ain* as a pattern in *rain,* a familiar word.
3. Next, she models the self-talk that she uses to try out the sounds from *rain* in the unfamiliar *stain.*
4. Then, she has the student try out the strategy on a series of unknown preselected words. These words share letter patterns with familiar words.
5. The teacher posts a set of model words that have common word patterns such as the *at* in *cat, ay* in *hay.* She uses picture clues next to the words to help readers remember the model word.
6. Thirty-three common word patterns are listed in the following box (Stahl, 1998).

ack	ain	ake	ale	all	ame	an	ank
ap	ash	at	ate	aw	ay		
eat	ell	est					
ice	ing	ink	ip	ir	ick	ide	
ight	ill	in	ine				
op	or	ore	ock	oke			
uck	ug	ump					

7. On a regular basis, the children read texts that contained words with familiar spelling patterns.

Further Applications

Basic View of Reading   Learning to read is an interactive process. By developing procedures to figure out words, the student uses the text first to sound out the word and then relates the new word to familiar words with the same language pattern.

Patterns of Strengths and Strategies   The word analogy strategy is most appropriate for students who can segment words into their sounds and match those sounds to the letters in the word. This technique builds on their strength and allows them to develop a system for decoding by analogy to key words.

Learner Patterns That Produce Increased Engagement

1. For a learner who can match sounds to letters, this technique helps develop a system for using what he knows to figure out new words.
*2. For a reader who readily uses what he knows but needs help focusing on letter pattern cues to figure out words, this technique matches the familiar with the unfamiliar in decoding words.
*3. For a passive learner who needs explanations to understand how to decode unfamiliar words, this technique provides a tool to build word recognition.

For Further Reading

Cunningham, P. M., & Allington, R. L. (2003). *Classrooms that work: They can all read and write* (3rd ed.). New York: Longman.

Gunning, T. G. (1998). *Assessing and correcting reading and writing difficulties.* Boston: Allyn & Bacon.

Stahl, S. (1998). Saying the "P" word: Nine guidelines for exemplary phonics instruction. In R. Allington (Ed.), *Teaching struggling readers* (pp. 208–216). Netwark, DE: International Reading Association.

Word Probe Strategy

Description   Word probe strategy is a structured phonics approach in which children are taught a strategic process of using key words to figure out unfamiliar words. The key words are displayed so the students can refer to them as they decode by analogy.

Text   Single words on word walls

Predominant Focus of Instruction

1. Processing focus: print
2. Instructional phase: skill lesson
3. Response mode emphasized: oral
4. Strategy emphasized: monitoring
5. Skill emphasized: word identification and word analysis
6. Source of information: text-based
7. Type of instruction: explicit

Procedure

1. The teacher explains reasons for learning about individual words such as:
   a. Using a picture of a cat to figure out the word *cat.*
   b. Using two cues such as a picture of a cat and the initial letter *k* to figure out the word *kitten.*
   c. Using all the letters and sounds to figure out a word, such as using *k-a-t* for *cat.*
2. The teacher models how to talk about the letters and sounds of the key words as they are introduced by saying, "I stretch out the word so I can hear all the sounds."
3. Next, she models holding up a finger for each sound in the word and counting the sounds in the word.
4. Then, the teacher models counting the letters in the word and matching the number of letters to the sounds.
5. The student repeats her model using the same self-talk with a key word or words and fills out the self-talk chart (Gaskins et al., 1996–1997).

TALK TO YOURSELF CHART

1. The word is _____.
2. Stretch the word. I hear _____ sounds.
3. I see _____ letters because _____.
4. The spelling pattern is _____.
5. This is what I know about the vowel _____.
6. Another word in the key word list with the same vowel sound is _____.

6. Each day the children read texts that contain words with familiar spelling patterns. They use the partner sharing chart or the making words chart as they work with partners in the classroom.
7. At the conclusion of each reading session, the student restates what he learned about language.
8. At home, the student tells his parents about the key word and talks aloud about how decoding works.
9. The parents write notes in the child's "What I Know About My Language" journal.

Further Applications

Basic View of Reading   Learning to read is an interactive process. By developing procedures to figure out words, the student uses the text first to sound out the word and then relates the new word to familiar words with the same language pattern.

Patterns of Strengths and Strategies   The word probe strategy is most appropriate for students who can segment words into their sounds and match those sounds to the letters in the word. This technique builds on their strengths and allows them to develop a system for decoding by analogy to key words.

Learner Patterns That Produce Increased Engagement

1. For a learner who can match some sounds to letters, this technique helps them develop a system for using what they know to figure out new words.
*2. For a reader who readily uses what he knows but needs help focusing on letter and sound cues to figure out words, this technique reinforces decoding words into sounds to increase recognition.
*3. For a passive learner who needs explicit explanations to understand the decoding process and how to use phonic knowledge when reading an unfamiliar word, this technique provides a tool for building word recognition.

For Further Reading
Gaskins, I. W., Ehri, L. C., Cress, C., O'Hara, C., & Donnelly, K. (1996–1997). Procedures for word learning: Making discoveries about words. *The Reading Teacher, 50,* 312–327.

■ Word Sorts

Targeted Reading Levels 1–4

Description   Word sorts are ways to sort word cards that enable the readers to share how they categorize words: for example, on the basis of similar letter patterns, word meanings, or grammatical functions. This technique uses target words to help students review and remember words by categorizing like characteristics.

Text   Isolated words

Predominant Focus of Instruction

1. Processing focus: print or meaning
2. Instructional phase: after reading
3. Response mode emphasized: oral
4. Strategy emphasized: elaboration
5. Skill emphasized: word identification or word meaning
6. Source of information: reader-based
7. Type of instruction: implicit

Procedure

1. The teacher or students select target words and write them on word cards.
2. Each student collects a box of personalized word cards drawn from language experience stories, basal readers, and/or trade books to form a word bank.
3. To start a lesson, the teacher asks the students to get out their word banks and form small groups or pairs.
4. The teacher demonstrates how to do a word sort by showing the words *one, two, six,* and *ten* and saying, "Why do you think these words go together?"
5. The students respond by saying, "They are numbers."
6. Then the teacher shows them three more word cards (*hat, rat, sat*) and asks, "Why so you think these words go together?"
7. The students respond that all the words have the letters *at* at the end.
8. The teacher explains the process of looking for like characteristics: some groups may have a meaning focus, some may have letter-sound focus, and others may have a grammatical focus such as *go, going, gone.* She asks the students to create groups of words that share the same characteristic (open word sort).
9. Each group explains how their words go together.
10. Next, the teacher directs all the groups to find words that share the same letter patterns.
11. Each group explains their categorizations.

Modification   For each group, the teacher can create a set of word cards that have similar letter patterns, word meanings, or grammatical functions. She asks the groups to arrange the cards according to the pattern and be able to tell how the words are alike. This word sort is closed because the teacher chooses the words to reinforce a concept that is being learned.

Further Applications

Basic View of Reading   Reading is a socio-interactive process in which learners share their thinking about how words are categorized based on their meaning, grapho-phonic similarity, or grammatical function. As students discuss how words are alike, they increase their active thinking.

Patterns of Strengths and Strategies   Word sorts are most appropriate for young readers who are developing a recognition vocabulary. For these students, categorizing words according to their distinctive features as well as their meaning enhances decoding by both meaning analogies and decoding analogies.

Learner Patterns That Produce Increased Engagement

1. For a learner who easily sees relationships but often does not look at the word patterns, this approach focuses the student on likenesses among words rather than on their differences.
2. For a social learner who learns more readily with a partner or in a group, this approach can be effective because his friends help him focus, in this case, on distinctive features that are alike in words.
*3. For a passive learner who needs to select key features so he can remember what the words look like, the sorting provides a tool for talking about how words look alike.

For Further Reading

Bear, D., Invernizzi, M., Templeton, S., & Johnston, F. (2004). *Words their way: Words study for phonics, vocabulary, and spelling instruction* (3rd ed.). Upper Saddle River, NJ: Merrill/Prentice Hall.

Roskos, K., & Walker, B. (1994). *Interactive handbook for understanding reading diagnosis.* Upper Saddle River, NJ: Merrill/Prentice Hall.

■ Word Walls

Description   Word walls are used to help readers develop their understanding of words. On large sheets of paper, the teacher writes critical and puzzling words for the students. The features of these words are discussed along with their meaning. Students can use the word walls when they write or read during classroom activities.

Text   Single words

Predominant Focus of Instruction

1. Processing focus: print
2. Instructional phase: before and after reading
3. Response mode emphasized: oral
4. Strategy emphasized: elaboration
5. Skill emphasized: word identification and word meaning
6. Source of information: reader-based
7. Type of instruction: implicit

Procedure

1. The teacher hangs a long sheet of paper on a wall and titles it, "Word Wall for _____." It could be a story, theme, or skill lesson.
2. The teacher introduces the word wall and writes key words for reading the story large enough for all students to read them.
3. After reading the teacher and students suggest other important story words and then write them on the word wall.
4. If students write the word on the wall, the teacher corrects spelling errors and discusses word features as students use these words when they write.
5. At this time, the teacher reviews spelling and word features as well as meaning.
6. For younger children, the teacher can add a small picture.
7. At the end of a unit, the teacher reviews all the words in the lesson, saying and spelling each word and putting it on an index card. The cards are collated on metal rings and put in the writing center.
8. The words can be sorted (see "Word Sorts") for phonic patterns. For example, all the words beginning with the same letter would be one sort, then rhyming words would be another sort, and so on.

Further Applications

Basic View of Reading   Learning to read means understanding words that influence stories. Readers need to use their knowledge of word features and word meanings to figure out story understanding; therefore, reading is an interactive process. By studying words, the students can elaborate their understanding of word meaning and word features.

Patterns of Strengths and Strategies   The word wall approach is most appropriate for students who learn word meaning and word features easily. This technique builds on their strength and allows them to develop a system for analyzing words.

Learner Patterns That Produce Increased Engagement

1. For a reader who readily uses what he knows and what's important to understanding new information, this technique promotes understanding the relationship words have to meaning.
*2. For a passive learner who needs help focusing on words to understand stories, this technique uses attention to meaning and word features to enhance reading.
*3. For a learner who can match sounds to letters but does not think about the meaning of individual words, this technique helps him develop a system for using what he knows to figure out word meaning and word features.

For Further Reading

Cunningham, P. M., & Cunningham, J. W. (1992). Making words: Enhancing the invented spelling-decoding connection. *The Reading Teacher, 46,* 106–107.

Snow, C. E., Burns, M. S., & Griffin, P. (1998). *Preventing reading difficulties in young children.* Washington, DC: National Academy Press.

Bibliography

Alexander, P., & Jetton, T. (2000). Learn from text: A multidimensional and developmental perspective. In M. Kamil, P. Mosenthal, P. D. Pearson, & R. Barr (Eds.), *Handbook of reading research* (Vol. 3, pp. 285–310). New York: Longman.

Allington, R. L. (1984). Oral reading. In P. D. Pearson (Ed.), *Handbook of reading research* (pp. 829–864). New York: Longman.

Allington, R. L. (1995). Literacy lessons in the elementary schools: Yesterday, today, and tomorrow. In R. L. Allington & S. A. Walmsley (Eds.), *No quick fix* (pp. 1–18). New York: Teachers College Press; Newark, DE: International Reading Association.

Allington, R. (2001). *What really matters for struggling readers: Designing research-based programs*. New York: Longman.

Allington, R. L., & Cunningham, P. M. (2002). *Schools that work: Where all children read and write* (2nd ed.). New York: HarperCollins.

Au, K. (1993). *Literacy instruction in multicultural settings*. Fort Worth, TX: Harcourt Brace Jovanovich.

Au, K. (2002). Multicultural factors and effective instruction of students of diverse backgrounds. In A. Farstrup & S. Samuels (Eds.), *What research has to say about reading instruction* (pp. 392–414). Newark, DE: International Reading Association.

Barr, R., Blachowicz, C., Katz, C., & Kaufman, B. (2005). *Reading diagnosis for teachers: An instructional approach* (4th ed.). White Plains, NY: Longman.

Barr, R., Blachowicz, C., & Wogman-Sadow, M. (1995). *Reading diagnosis for teachers: An instructional approach* (3rd ed.). White Plains, NY: Longman.

Bear, D., Invernizzi, M., Templeton, S., & Johnston, F. (2004). *Words their way: Word study for phonics, vocabulary, and spelling instruction* (3rd ed.). Upper Saddle River, NJ: Merrill/Prentice Hall.

Bromley, K. D. (1996). *Webbing with literature: Creating story maps with children's books* (2nd ed.). Boston: Allyn & Bacon.

Clay, M. M. (1993). *Reading recovery: A guidebook for teachers in training*. Portsmouth, NH: Heinemann.

Cunningham, P. M., & Allington, R. L. (2003). *Classrooms that work: They can all read and write* (3rd ed.). New York: Longman.

Cunningham, P. M., & Cunningham, J. W. (1992). Making words: Enhancing the invented spelling-decoding connection. *The Reading Teacher, 46,* 106–107.

DeCarlo, J. E. (1995). *Perspectives in whole language*. Boston: Allyn & Bacon.

Duffy, G. G., & Roehler, L. R. (1987). Teaching reading skills as strategies. *The Reading Teacher, 40,* 414–418.

Duke, N., & Pearson, P. D. (2002). Effective practices for developing reading comprehension. In A. Farstrup & S. Samuels (Eds.), *What research has to say about reading instruction* (pp. 205–242). Newark, DE: International Reading Association.

Dybdahl, C. S., & Walker, B. J. (1996). *Prediction strategies and comprehension instruction.* Unpublished paper, University of Alaska, Anchorage, AK.

Fountas, I. C., & Pinnell, G. S. (1996). *Guided reading: Good first teaching for all children.* Portsmouth, NH: Heinemann.

Gambrell, L. B., & Jawitz, P. B. (1993). Mental imagery, text illustrations, and children's story comprehension and recall. *Reading Research Quarterly, 28,* 264–276.

Gambrell, L., & Marinak, B. A. (1997). Incentive and instrinsic motivation to read. In J. T. Guthrie & A. Wigfield (Eds.), *Reading engagement: Motivating readers through integrated instruction* (pp. 205–217). Newark, DE: International Reading Association.

Gaskins, I. W., Ehri, L. C., Cress, C., O'Hara, C., & Donnelly, K. (1996–1997). Procedures for word learning: Making discoveries about words. *The Reading Teacher, 50,* 312–327.

Gillet, J., & Temple, C. (1994). *Understanding reading problems* (4th ed.). Glenview, IL: Scott Foresman.

Gipe, J. P. (2002). *Multiple paths to literacy: Classroom techniques for struggling readers* (5th ed.). Upper Saddle River, NJ: Merrill/Prentice Hall.

Glazer, S. M. (1992). *Reading comprehension: Self-monitoring strategies to develop independent readers.* New York: Scholastic.

Glodenberg, C. (1992–1993). Instructional conversations: Promoting comprehension through discussion. *The Reading Teacher, 46,* 316–326.

Goodman, K. (1996). Principles of revaluing. In Y. M. Goodman & A. M. Marek (Eds.), *Retrospective miscue analysis: Revaluing readers and reading* (pp. 13–21). Katonah, NY: Richard C. Owen Publishers.

Goodman, Y. M., & Marek, A. M. (1996). Retrospective miscue analysis. In Y. M. Goodman & A. M. Marek (Eds.), *Retrospective miscue analysis: Revaluing readers and reading* (pp. 39–49). Katonah, NY: Richard C. Owen Publishers.

Goswami, U. (2000). Phonological and lexical processes. In M. Kamil, P. Mosenthal, P. D. Pearson, & R. Barr (Eds.), *Handbook of reading research* (Vol. 3, pp. 251–268). New York: Longman.

Gunning, T. G. (1998). *Assessing and correcting reading and writing difficulties.* Boston: Allyn & Bacon.

Johns, J. L. (2001) *Basic reading inventory* (8th Ed.). Dubuque, IA: Kendall-Hunt.

Johns, J. L., & Lenski, S. (2001). *Improving reading: A handbook of strategies* (3rd ed.). Dubuque, IA: Kendall-Hunt.

Johnston, P. H., & Allington, R. (1991). Remediation. In R. Barr, M. Kamil, P. Mosenthal, & P. D. Pearson (Eds.), *Handbook of reading research* (Vol. 2, pp. 984–1012). New York: Longman.

Jordan, A. (1989). *Diagonostic narrative.* Unpublished journals of lessons. Eastern Montana College.

Juel, C. (1988). Learning to read and write: A longitudinal study of 54 children from first through fourth grades. *Journal of Educational Psychology, 80,* 437–447.

Juel, C. (1998). What kind of one-on-one tutoring helps a poor reader? In C. Hulme & R. M. Joshi (Eds.), *Reading and spelling: Development and disorders* (pp. 449–472). Mahwah, NJ: Lawrence Erlbaum.

Kaufman, A. S., & Kaufman, N. L. (1983). *K-ABC Kaufman assessment battery for children: Interpretive manual.* Circle Pines: MN: American Guidance Services.

Macon, J. M., Bawell, D., & Vogt, M. (1991). Responses to literature: Grades K–8. Newark, DE: International Reading Association.

Manzo, A., & Manzo, V. (1990). *Content area reading: A heuristic approach.* Upper Saddle River, NJ: Merrill/Prentice Hall.

McCormick, S. (1992). Disabled readers' erroneous responses to inferential comprehension questions: Description and analysis. *Reading Research Quarterly, 27,* 54–77.

McCormick, S. (2003). *Instructing students who have literacy problems* (4th ed.). Upper Saddle River, NJ: Merrill/Prentice Hall.

Mokhtari, K., & Reichard, C. (2002). Assessing students' metacognitive awareness of reading strategies. *Journal of Educational Psychology, 94*(2), 240–259.

Morrow, L., & Walker, B. (1997). *The reading team: A handbook for volunteer tutors K–3.* Newark, DE: International Reading Association.

Paris, S. G., Lipson, M. Y., & Wixson, K. K. (1994). Becoming a strategic reader. In R. B. Ruddell, M. R. Ruddell, & H. Singer (Eds.), *Theoretical models and processes of reading* (4th ed., pp. 788–811). Newark, DE: International Reading Association.

Powell, W. R. (1981). *The finger count system for monitoring reading behavior.* Unpublished Paper. University of Florida, Gainesville, FL.

Pressley, M. (2000). What should comprehension instruction be the instruction of? In M. Kamil, P. Mosenthal, P. D. Pearson, & R. Barr (Eds.), *Handbook of reading research* (Vol. 3, pp. 525–544). New York: Longman.

Rasinski, T. (1999). Making and writing words. *Reading Online,* Retrieved September 1, 2002 from http://readingonline.org/articles/words/rasinski.html.

Rasinski, T. (2001). Making and writing words using letter patterns. *Reading Online,* Retrieved September 1, 2002, from http://readingonline.org/articles/rasinski/MWW-LP.html.

Rasinski T., & Padak, N. (2004). *Effective reading strategies: Teaching children who find reading difficult* (3rd ed.). Upper Saddle River, NJ.: Merrill/Prentice Hall.

Rasinski, T., & Padak, N. (2001) *From phonics to fluency: Effective teaching of decoding and reading fluency in the elementary school.* Boston, MA: Allyn & Bacon.

Reutzel, D. R., & Cooter, R. (2004). *Strategies for reading assessment and instruction: Helping every child succeed* (4th ed.). Upper Saddle River, NJ: Merrill/Prentice Hall.

Roskos, K., & Walker, B. J. (1994). *Interactive handbook for understanding reading diagnosis.* Upper Saddle River, NJ: Merrill/Prentice Hall.

Roskos, K., & Walker, B. (1998). *Teachers' understanding and adaptation of their discourse as instructional conversation through self-assessment activity.* Paper presented at the annual meeting of the American Education Research Association, San Diego, CA.

Ruddell, M. R. (2005). *Teaching content reading and writing* (4th ed.). Hoboken, NJ: Wiley Publishers.

Ruddell, R. B., & Unrau, N. J. (1994). Reading as a meaning-construction process: The reader, the text, and the teacher. In R. B. Ruddell, M. R. Ruddell, & H. Singer (Eds.), *Theoretical models and processes of reading* (4th ed., pp. 996–1056). Newark, DE: International Reading Association.

Ruddell, R. B., & Unrau, N. J. (1997). The role of responsive teaching in focusing reader intention and developing reader motivation. In J. T. Guthrie & A. Wigfield (Eds.), *Reading engagement: Motivating readers through integrated instruction* (pp. 102–127). Newark, DE: International Reading Association.

Schunk, D. H., & Zimmerman, B. J. (1997). Developing self-efficacious readers and writers: The role of social and self-regulary processes. In J. T. Guthrie & A. Wigfield (Eds.), *Reading engagement: Motivating readers through integrated instruction* (pp. 34–50). Newark, DE: International Reading Association.

Short, K. G., Harste, J. C., & Burke, C. (1996). *Creating classrooms for authors and inquirers.* Portsmouth, NH: Heinemann.

Snow, C. E., Burns, M. S., & Griffin, P. (1998). *Preventing reading difficulties in young children.* Washington, DC: National Academy Press.

Spiegel, D. L. (1998). Silver bullets, babies, and bath water: Literature response groups in a balanced literacy program. *The Reading Teacher, 52,* 114–124.

Stahl, S. (1998). Saying the "P" word: Nine guidelines for exemplary phonics instruction. In R. Allington (Ed.), *Teaching struggling readers* (pp. 208–216). Netwark, DE: International Reading Association.

Standards for the English Language Arts. (1996). International Reading Association and National Council for the Teachers of English. Newark, DE: International Reading Association and Urbana, Ill: National Council of Teachers of English.

Stanovich, K. E. (1986). Mathew effects in reading: Some consequences of individual differences in the acquisition of literacy. *Reading Research Quarterly, 21,* 360–406.

Taylor, B., Harris, L., Pearson, P. D., & Garcia, G. (1995). *Reading difficulties: Instruction and assessment.* New York: McGraw-Hill.

Taylor, B., Pearson, P. D., Clark, K., & Walpole, S. (2002). Effective schools and accomplished teachers: Lessons about primary grade reading instruction in low-income schools. In B. Taylor & P. D. Pearson (Eds.), *Teaching reading: Effective schools, accomplished teachers* (pp. 3–72). Mahwah, NJ: Lawrence Erlbaum.

Tierney, R. J., & Readence, J. E. (2005). *Reading strategies and practices: A compendium* (6th ed.). Boston: Allyn & Bacon.

Tompkins, G. E. (2004). *Fifty literacy strategies: Step by step* (2nd ed.). Upper Saddle River, NJ: Merrill/Prentice Hall.

Topping, K. (1989). Peer tutoring and paired reading: Combining two powerful techniques. *The Reading Teacher, 42,* 488–494.

Vygotsky, L. S. (1978). *Mind in society.* Cambridge, MA: Harvard University Press.

Walker, B. J. (1990). *What research says to the teacher: Remedial reading.* Washington, DC: National Education Association.

Walker, B. J. (2003). *Supporting struggling readers* (2nd ed.). Markham, Ontario: Pippin Publishing.

Watson, D., & Hoge, S. (1993). Reader-selected miscues. In Y. M. Goodman & A. M. Marck (Eds.), *Retrospective miscue analysis: Revalving readers & reading* (pp. 157–164). Katonah, KY: Richard C. Owen Publishers.

Yopp, H. (1995). A test for assessing phonemic awareness in young children. *The Reading Teacher, 49,* 20–29.

Zutell, J. (1988, May). *Developing a procedure for assessing oral reading fluency: Establishing validity and reliability.* Paper presented at 33rd Annual Convention, International Reading Association, Toronto, Canada.

Zutell, J., & Rasinski, T. (1991). Training teachers to attend to their students' oral reading fluency. *Theory to Practice, 30* (3), 211–217.

Index